In over 70 years as a photographer he has travelled more than 2 million miles and taken thousands of photographs. His photographs have appeared in practically all the world's leading newspapers and magazines as well as his nine previous books on Royal Families.

He was made a Fellow of the Masters Association, a Fellow of The British Institute of Professional Photographers, a Fellow of the Royal Photographic Society. In 1978 was conferred with the Insignia of Taj by His Imperial Majesty the Shah of Iran and in 2008 was awarded an MBE.

Previous titles by Reginald Davis:

ROYALTY OF THE WORLD (1969)
PRINCESS ANNE A GIRL OF OUR TIME (1973)
ELIZABETH OUR QUEEN (1977)
ROYAL FAMILIES OF THE WORLD (1978)
THE PRINCE OF WALES (1978)
MONARCHY IN POWER (1979)
THE PERSIAN PRINCE (1979)
THE ROYAL FAMILY OF THAILAND (1981)
THE ROYAL FAMILY OF LUXEMBOURG (1989)

I dedicate this book to my darling wife Audrey, without whom it would not be possible.
To my loving children Marilyn and Jonathan, and my grandchildren Nicholas, Elliot and James.

Reginald Davis MBE

MY LIFE PHOTOGRAPHING ROYALTY AND THE FAMOUS

A CIP catalogue record for this title is available from the British Library.

ISBN 9781787109681 (Hardback)
ISBN 9781787109698 (E-Book)

www.austinmacauley.com

First Published (2017)
Austin Macauley Publishers Ltd.
25 Canada Square
Canary Wharf
London
E14 5LQ

I would wish to offer my sincere thanks to Her Majesty Queen Elizabeth, Her Royal Highness the Princess Royal, Queen Sophie of Spain, Queen Beatrix of The Netherlands, Queen Paola of Belgium, The Grand Ducal Family of Luxembourg, Queen Sirikit of Thailand, Empress Farah of Iran, Sophia Loren, Princess Ira von Furstenberg , Isabella Rosselini, and Dame Joan Collins.

My name is Reginald Davis.

I was born in London on 5th March 1925. My parents were called Sydney and Hannah. I had three sisters: Maisie, Phyllis and, the only survivor, my younger sister Delia.

As a youngster I lived in North London and when the war broke out my parents moved to St. Albans. I was evacuated to Cambridge and went to school at Emanuel College. When I eventually left Cambridge for my home, I joined the St. Albans Sea Cadets and achieved the privilege of becoming Head Sea Cadet.

I was called up on 17th March 1943 to the Royal Navy and sent to Skegness, – Butlins, the original holiday camp, named HMS Royal Arthur.

At HMS Royal Arthur, I was being trained as a signalman dealing with flags and Morse code. We were asked, "If anyone is interested in photography, they should report to the First Lieutenant's office." I thought, 'If I am going to survive the war, what would I be doing in signals or Morse?' Therefore I decided that if I was a photographer at least I would have a profession when the war ended and so I reported to the office.

After six weeks of training at HMS Royal Arthur I was transferred to the Fleet Air Arm and had photographic training at Bognor under the supervision of the RAF photo division. As part of my training, I had to fly in an Anson aircraft and lay down in the nose of the plane, which was all in perspex, an unbreakable glass, taking photographs. It was rather scary – as if I was a bird and all I could see was land and sea.

Having passed my exams, I then became a Fleet Air Arm photographer and went to the Royal Naval air base at Yeovilton before being sent to Greenock in Scotland, HMS Waxwing. I waited there before boarding a troopship that was sailing to Bombay. We had all different nationals on board – Americans, Canadians and West Indians – and a few women. The ship was called The Maloya and was an Indian vessel. From Bombay, we were transferred again to a Polish vessel of 6,000 tonnes en-route to Colombo, Ceylon (now Sri Lanka), and the heavy seas made nearly everyone on board sick, except myself and a few of my friends.

Now in Colombo, stationed on the racecourse (no horses,) – the name of our base was HMS Bherunda. The photographic section consisted of six, with an officer in charge. I was there for about five months, sleeping in the stand on the benches. My work consisted of processing films, printing photographs and making mosaics for the instructions for the pilots who were bombing and strafing the Nicobar Islands and the oil fields of Sumatra. It was here I caught dinghy, which is a form of malaria, and was hospitalised. I recovered after five or six days. On the base I had a first cousin who was a doctor, a Lieutenant Doctor Morris Morton, and we went out in the evenings together on many occasions.

My time had now come to join the aircraft carrier HMS Victorious, a beautiful ship of some 23,000 tonnes. I was assigned as a photographer to 1836 Squadron, one of the two Corsair squadrons on board (fighters). Also there were two bomber squadrons of Avenger aircraft. The work was quite similar to what I had been doing, plus loading and fitting cameras to the aircraft. Each aircraft had a vertical camera, one oblique on the side of the fuselage and, of course, the pilot's firing camera. It was also my duty as a member of the ship's company to be on the Captain's bridge at times for photographing the landing and taking off of the aircraft in case of any mishaps, and there were quite a few.

Corsairs on the flight deck of HMS Victorious

HMS Victorious hit by a Japanese Kamekazi

11

We operated in the Indian Ocean for many months and attacked the oilfields at Palembang in Sumatra, whilst Japanese Zero aircraft attacked us daily. HMS Illustrious was the first of our carriers to be hit – she was about one mile away from us. Then we were hit and slightly damaged, sustaining few casualties. There were long periods at sea without seeing the sight of land. Provisions and mail were brought aboard from a destroyer by breeches buoy and we were also refuelled. We then sailed south to Sydney, Australia; we were all excited knowing the ship was going in for a refit for several weeks and we would be sent to a land base during this time. The crossing of the Great Australian Bight from Freemantle to Sydney was quite harrowing with the swelling seas.

On arrival in Sydney we were sent to a base some 30 minutes outside the city named Parramatta, and the food we were given was simply wonderful. And so my colleagues and I spent a lovely two weeks of relaxation, more or less on holiday.

Back to the ship, sailing north to join the American 6th Fleet under the command of Admiral Nimitz at Leyte in the Philippines. In our British Fleet, we had our sister ship, HMS Illustrious, accompanied by HMS Formidable and HMS Indomitable. Sailing at the stern of each carrier was a destroyer for picking up pilots who may have had to ditch their aircraft through damage or lack of fuel. Then we were told one evening at a lovely sunset on the calm blue sea that the following morning we were going into action off the island of Okinawa in support of the American task force invading the island. Many of us were quite scared and wondered what sort of action we may encounter. I know we all prayed and thought of home and our families.

On board the ship the only weapons I had were the cameras and my lifebelt. Being a photographer, it was really left up to me to take the most advantageous position at action stations. I had access to roam the ship at will. There were three other photographers on board and our section was below the waterline. When action stations sounded, if you were off duty you would be in the photographic compartment, and whilst in action the hatch above would be sealed until after the all-clear. However, if we were hit by a torpedo, one could not get out and this was quite a danger. Fortunately we were not hit.

Morning came and action stations were sounded. We were in the middle of a Japanese onslaught off Okinawa. Kamikaze aircraft were all round the fleet, like bees around a honey pot. The noise of the oerlikon guns and the 4.5-inch guns shelling coupled with the screeching of aircraft was deafening; many aircraft fell into the sea, both theirs and ours. The gunners wore their anti-flash gear and everyone wore lifebelts. In those days a lifebelt was a circular tube of navy material which one would blow up like a balloon.

Japanese zeroes were coming in low and fast and hitting our ships – it was hell. On VE day (Victory in Europe Day) our ship was hit twice by Kamikaze zeros and we lost many lives. But we remained operational. I remember one kamikaze hit us forward – our deck was 4-inch" steel – and it made a huge hole tearing the metal apart. I was photographing on the flight deck and saw the sky full of white smoke from the fighting. It was indeed a terrible day. The American carriers had wooden decks that easily caught fire, but we had decks made of steel which was more protective. After action stations it was peaceful once again and we had a church service for thanksgiving –

We returned to Leyte, our base in the Pacific for a few days' rest and replenishments. Then back into action again. For the next month or so we saw nothing but sea and action and we were down to eating corn beef, biscuits, potatoes and onions. We were told that we were 36 miles off the coast of Japan. News came through that an Atom bomb had just been dropped by the Americans and we cheered as we knew the war would soon finish. And so it did. What a wonderful, wonderful relief, with excitement all round.

We sailed back to Sydney. We were alive. We then headed home; it took six weeks to sail into Portsmouth. Our ship was dressed overall and the crowds cheered on the dockside as we entered the port. I left HMS Victorious and was sent to Padstow in Cornwall, a shore-based establishment named HMS Vulture. There, I was demobbed.

I remember coming home with yards of yellow parachute silk as a gift for one of my sisters. I was met at St. Albans station by my uncle who drove me to my home where all the family were waiting to greet me. It was most exciting.

My service life helped me in civilian life because I became a professional photographer, photographing the Queen and the royal family over the next 50 years.

At the end of hostilities I was awarded the 1939-1945 Star, the Burma Star and Pacific Clasp, and the Victory medal.

In civilian life I was decorated in 1978 with the Order of Taj by His Imperial Majesty the Shah of Iran for services to photography and in 2008 I was decorated by Her Majesty the Queen with the MBE.

After being demobbed in 1946 and going into civilian life, I joined a small Fleet Street press agency called Dominion Press. It was there that I started my professional career. I covered the photography for most commercial and press stories. During that time, I was sent to Northolt airport with a colleague to photograph a group of Russians arriving; on our way a plane had crash-landed on to the roof of two houses. We ignored the Russians and took photographs of the crashed plane instead. Incidentally, the pilot was safe. We were so excited about taking those pictures that we decided, on the way back to the office, to stop at a local pub and have a drink to celebrate. By the time we got back to the office, pictures had already been published from other sources and we nearly got the sack.

Later I was seconded by Dominion Press to a film company owned by the Boulting brothers who were making the film *Brighton Rock* in 1947 with Richard Attenborough. I was sent to Brighton to arrange darkroom facilities as I was employed as a publicity photographer, and it was on one of those days that I met a girl named Audrey whom I was introduced to on the beach by an old friend. It was Audrey whom I eventually married in 1948. We were blessed with one daughter, Marilyn, who married Dr. Jonathan Warren in 1977. We now have three grandsons – Nicholas, Elliot and James – and a great granddaughter, Phoebe.

After *Brighton Rock*, the Boulting brothers were impressed with my work and offered to put me on their staff at the amazing salary of £15 per week. The next film I worked on was *The Guinea Pig* and that followed a trip to Italy for a film called *Private Angelo* with Peter Ustinov. On returning to England after four months in Italy, the film industry was in turmoil, and I and many others were made redundant. It was then that I started on my own, photographing anything commercial and industrial. My wife and I set up a darkroom in a spare room in our flat.

We hired a typewriter for seven shillings and sixpence per week and wrote to several organisations. 1951 came with the British exhibition and I was able to take various photographs on commission. I was also commissioned by the *Nursing Mirror* to take photographs of nurses' prize-givings. On one occasion I photographed the birth of a baby at the *British* Hospital for Mothers and Babies in Woolwich. It was there that the matron had me capped and gowned and called me Dr. Davis, as the patient was aware that I was in attendance since this was her third birth.

I added the *Daily Express* to my work, photographing in the evenings from 6pm until the early hours as a freelancer, being sent to premiers, parties, a plane crash in Surrey, a train crash in Putney, and all types of stories. It was on one of these evenings in 1959 that I was sent to the Hyde Park Hotel as a 'rota' photographer (representing all the newspapers). The Queen was attending the annual ball of the Lancers. I had two photos to take for the rota in black and white. Having taken these photos, I loaded my camera with colour film and took five pictures of the Queen. The result was fantastic and *Queen Magazine* published those on the front page and inside and handed me a large cheque.

I worked at the *Daily Express* in the evenings and did my commercial work during the day. I also enjoyed photographing at nurses' prize-givings. One Christmas Eve I was photographing the nurses singing carols in a ward in Hampstead Hospital, and as I stood on a chair to get extra height the chair slipped. I fell, but kept hold of my camera to save damaging it; I broke two ribs and became a hospital patient.

I always used to keep my cameras loaded in the boot of my car in case I came across an incident. On one such occasion I needed my camera when the Brent Cross bridge on the fly over collapsed onto a passing coach. I had a telephone call from the *Evening Standard* informing me of the accident and that I should promptly go to the scene. Several people were killed. I took my camera out, without checking if it had film, and started taking photos. Unbeknown to me – and having had a late night at the Daily Express – I had forgotten to load the film. Consequently, the roll of film that I gave to the dispatch rider had not taken up on the spool and I had no pictures. I was absolutely devastated. That was in 1964.

In 1969, when I had my first book published, *Royalty of the World* I had a local newspaper writer and photographer visit me. They said, "A local photographer took photos of the Brent Cross crash five years ago and he had no pictures on his film."

I said, "Yes, and that was me," and we all laughed. These things do happen from time to time.

On a state visit the Queen always meets the press on the first day of the visit. On one occasion, in 1961 in India, the reception was immediately after visiting the Gandhi shrine. On visiting the shrine we had to remove our shoes – and many of the Indian press had holes in their socks. It was rather funny as, after the ceremony, we all had to rush back to our transport and several of the guys forgot their shoes and had to dash back to get them. At the reception we were split up into small groups and then presented to the Queen. We were told to talk with her and, rather nervously with my hand behind my back, I said, "Did you enjoy the flight Ma'am?"

She replied, "One can never really enjoy flying; you are never relaxed."

Prince Philip, jovial as ever, followed in the Queen's footsteps, came over to us and enquired if any of us had been to India before. I really put my foot in it when I replied, "I have, during the war."

Philip said, "How long were you here for?"

"Well," I replied, "I was only in Bombay for one day, sir." I was interrupted with great laughter, with the Prince nearly falling over himself laughing. My face must have been the colour of a post box as I interrupted the laughter, saying, "I had been to Ceylon for five months and that country is very similar to India."

Queen Elizabeth riding an Elephant

I was photographing Prince Philip with his children, Charles and Anne, when they visited the Acropolis in Athens, when he said to me, "Haven't you finished yet? You will run out of film. I feel sorry for the poor amateurs if the professionals haven't got enough pictures after all this time."

When in Athens I photographed the wedding of King Constantine of Greece to Princess Anne Marie of Denmark.

I had photographed 14 royal weddings in seven countries. The wedding in Greece was colourful; the venue was the Metropolitan Cathedral. The bride and groom stood in front of the Bishop as he held a crown over their heads, as is the tradition, and ceremoniously announced their marriage.

King Carl Gustav of Sweden married Sylvia Sommerlath in Stockholm. The outdoor scene was spectacular as they walked from Drottningholm Palace on a red carpet to an awaiting boat. Crowds lining the grounds had a line of violinists playing in front of them dressed in lederhosen and tyrolean hats.

Of course, nothing matched the wedding of Prince Charles to Lady Diana Spencer. The wedding was watched by millions around the world as he kissed his bride on the balcony of Buckingham Palace. Apart from that scene, I was fortunate enough to take a photograph inside St. Paul's Cathedral of Lady Diana Spencer walking down the aisle on the arm of her father. In the third row of the congregation, as she passed, was Camilla Parker-Bowles looking on. That was a most memorable picture.

Diana Spencer walking down the aisle on the arm of her father

Princess Margaret and Lord Snowdon took a short holiday in Sardinia and I was commissioned by a magazine to photograph the couple. I arrived at the Costa Smeralda, parked my car – leaving my equipment – and walked into the bar of the hotel. Their detective came up to me. He was surprised I was there and asked me where my cameras were. I politely told him that I had left them in the car. He then told me to get them. I left, collected them and proceeded back to the outside of the bar when Lord Snowdon came up to me and said, "You can take your pictures when we walk down to the yacht." Princess Margaret and her husband, who was carrying water skies, were with their friends, the Guinesses, and it made a very pleasant holiday picture. They boarded their yacht and waved to me as they sailed away.

The Aga Khan was another famous person that I had the honour to photograph when I was in Sardinia photographing Princess Margaret and Lord Snowdon. He invited me on his yacht which was in the harbour. He asked me how I got on with my pictures of the Princess; I spent a very happy hour with him and enjoyed a drink before leaving.

A totally different assignment occurred when I went to Saigon in Vietnam in 1967 when the war was at its height. My wife didn't want me to go. However, I was assigned by an Italian magazine for an exclusive photo audience with Madame Nguyễn Cao Kỳ, wife of South Vietnam's Premier, Marshal Kỳ. She arrived by helicopter, wearing a flight suit, for my exclusive photo session at her home in the centre of a grimly fortified military base in a Saigon suburb. Added to the usual difficulties, on that occasion was the saturating humidity in a temperature of 100 degrees Fahrenheit, and the fact that I had been kept awake several nights by the ceaseless pounding of the guns in that unhappy city. While I photographed her, the 26 year-old Madame Kỳ talked sadly about the war. "I have been to the front many times," she told me, "and I have seen all the horrors of the war, the killings, the wounded and all the suffering. So much of my time is devoted to helping our country's efforts and to relieving some of the distress." I was pleased to leave Saigon and had a few days' relaxation in Bangkok before flying home.

When Churchill died I was commissioned to photograph him lying in state in Westminster Hall. I also flew in a helicopter over London, showing the enormous crowds queuing all the way along the embankment. It was a tremendous sight. The door of the aircraft was taken off which gave me more versatility, and I was strapped in for safety. I know the heavy winds and the noise of the plane were deafening. Nonetheless, I was successful with the results. An earlier time, I photographed him at the French Embassy in London when he attended a banquet with the Queen and Prince Philip. As they were leaving the Embassy the Queen stepped into her car and sat in the far corner. I was crouching down and moving closer into the open doorway to take a photograph of her when a voice behind me said, "You will be inside the car if you move any closer." That happened to be Prince Philip as he was saying goodnight to Churchill. I felt very embarrassed; nonetheless, I got the photograph I wanted.

Winston Churchill

In 1968, flying with the Queen, we flew in a British Airways 'Comet' aircraft from Rio de Janeiro to Santiago in Chile. The seating was backwards to the engine, supposedly for safety, we were told. We were served with gilt crockery and silver cutlery. In Brasilia, the capital of Brazil, the whole city was a mass of mosquitoes and we were all badly bitten. I remember Prince Philip introducing me to the President, and to my embarrassment he said, "This is Reg, our Christmas tree, we call him that as he has so many cameras round his neck."

My colleague Freddie Reid of the *Daily Mirror* and I were staying in a small hotel in a one-eyed Indian village, some one hour's flight from Picton in the Andes. The hotel barman had never seen an Englishman before and was so excited when we ordered a gin and tonic, he poured the gin nearly to the brim and put in hardly any tonic. We drank this, then ordered our meal, but only got as far as the soup. The following day we took a small aircraft – piloted by a pilot who was worse-for-wear after drinking the night before – to where the Queen would be relaxing during a break from the state visit. The plane wobbled quite a bit on the journey but fortunately we arrived safely.

The Queen had a weekend break from the state occasion and the Chilean government arranged for Her Majesty and the Duke to relax in Picton. We joined quite a number of Chilean photographers who had gathered for a possible photo session. The Queen and Prince Philip, with their hosts, were seated in deck chairs with the mountains in the background. It was a very informal picturesque setting, but unfortunately the Chilean photographers were trying to take a very low angle picture which appeared to be showing the Queen's legs and the session immediately ceased. We flew all that way and back to our destination for a photo call that lasted just three minutes, all because of the Chilean photographers.

It has just come to mind that on a state visit to Austria back in 1968 I heard the Queen swear. She was attending a diplomatic reception in a Viennese palace. It was quite cold as she came into the room and the hosts weren't there at that moment. Irritated, the Queen shouted to her flunkies who were standing at the door, "Shut that bloody door!" she didn't seem to be in a very happy frame of mind that day, and I'd never seen flunkies move so quickly.

One April morning in 1969, I was invited to Frogmore at Windsor Castle. There I was to photograph the Queen and the royal family in the gardens. For days I had been wondering how to take these pictures. I barely had time to arrange my equipment, and for a picture I had in mind I needed a rug or carpet as the early morning grass was damp. A Persian carpet was found and I laid it down in front of the lake. The Queen and her family came towards me and my first reaction was to wonder how she always managed to look so radiant. I bowed and politely asked if they would sit on the carpet. Prince Philip remarked, "Whatever is a Persian carpet doing in the middle of Windsor?"

I said, "I wouldn't want your bottoms to get wet from the early morning dew, sir." I thought they were going to refuse at first when I suggested the whole family sit on the carpet. For a split second nothing happened, then the Queen turned to Prince Andrew and Prince Edward and said, "Come along, children, let's sit on the magic carpet and fly away."

The Queen has a great aura. It's difficult to define, but it comes over you in waves. She was very kind that day – she sensed the situation, put me at ease and said, "I feel sorry for you because there are six of us and only one of you." Then I took some shots of Prince Philip with the young princes. Prince Edward climbed on to his lap and Prince Andrew leant against the back of a bench. You've got to be very tactful when you ask for anything, or even make a suggestion. I therefore leave my most powerful ideas until the end of a session so if I'm turned down I know that I'm covered by the pictures I've already taken.

Queen Elizabeth and her family on a Persian carpet

While I was at Frogmore I asked the Queen, "Is Prince Andrew heavy?"

She looked at me enquiringly and promptly replied, "Good gracious, yes."

"And what about Prince Edward?" I continued.

She smiled and said, "What have you in mind?"

"I wonder if it is possible for you to give Prince Edward a swing towards my camera?" I replied. I knew if I could pull that shot off it would be one of the most unusual sets of informal pictures ever taken of the royal family. "Come along, Anne, you and I will do it," she said briskly, and they began swinging Prince Edward to and fro.

If that had been declined I would have lost my most powerful picture. If I'd approached the subject at the beginning of the session it would have killed the rest of the sitting. I took a sequence of seven pictures, all of which were approved by Buckingham Palace for publication and were published all over the world.

The Queen and Princess Anne giving Prince Edward a swing

On an earlier occasion, in 1971, I was flying with Prince Charles and Princess Anne with the press corps to Nairobi, Kenya. They came along the aircraft and talked to us. It was on this trip that we went on a safari tour and also met President Jomo Kenyatta, who always carried a fly swatter. The safari was a three-day event, during which time Prince Charles was unshaven.

Prince Charles on safari.

Also in 1971 I flew to Tokyo, 14 hours over the pole on a British Airways flight. Arriving tired at my hotel I was informed by a message awaiting that a member of the Japanese foreign office would be meeting me and that I would be escorted by train up-country on a two hour journey to Nasu Palace. The train was packed with noisy people shouting and eating and it smelled like raw fish. It was indeed a most uncomfortable and unpleasant journey. On arrival at the hotel, the only one in the town, we were told there was only one room available but that it had twin beds. I had no alternative but to share this with my Japanese aide. I was extremely anti-Japanese, since I had been in the Far East during the war, where we encountered kamikaze aircraft diving on our ships and killing many sailors. As I lay on the bed trying to fall asleep, the thoughts of those suicide bombers attacking our fleet were buzzing in my mind. I woke with the sun streaming into our room and suddenly realised I would be meeting the Emperor today – a man who was accused of war crimes.

We were taken by car to the summer palace and I was hurriedly ushered to the corner of a garden where a number of courtiers were awaiting, like I was, the presence of the Emperor and his wife. It may be easier with European royalty, but protocol in Japan was still very strict. Emperor Hirohito may no longer have been regarded as divine, but his courtiers had precise ideas as to how their monarch should be approached.

I was invited to photograph the Emperor and Empress in the summer palace at Nasu. I was informed that I must not speak to the Emperor or the Empress and to take the photos with the mountain in the background within 10 minutes. I totally ignored everything that was said and, as the Emperor descended the steps into the garden, I said, "Good morning." He held out his hand to shake mine. I then walked with the Emperor and Empress and showed them where I would like them to stand. This was beside a tree surrounded by waist-high grass, a perfect setting which reminded me of the Burma jungle, where the Japanese tortured many soldiers building the railway. The pictures were dignified and no one would guess the motive. Later I photographed them holding some of their favourite birds and standing in heavy undergrowth.

The Emperor said to me, "You are the only non-Japanese ever to have photographed me."

I said to him, "I have flown 14 hours and two hours on a train to see you." He smiled and the session was over. It lasted 19 minutes. The courtiers were critical about the way their monarchs were treated.

"Well, they're not gods," I said, "and even God you sometimes speak to." The *Daily Mail* published the pictures when Their Majesties arrived in England and splashed them across their centre pages.

Emperor Hirohito and Empress Nagako

I continued my journey from Tokyo to Tel Aviv; it was here in Israel that I was going to have a photo session with Golda Meir, the warrior of the middle-east, the grand old lady herself. I met with Golda Meir in her home in Jerusalem. She had her grandchildren with her which made the session even more interesting. The photo session was on a Saturday afternoon, the Jewish Sabbath. She smoked cigarettes, one after the other. To try and relax the children and to get them cosied up to their grandmother, I said, "Why don't you cuddle up to your grandmother?" They did, and her granddaughter poured her a coffee. After a very pleasant afternoon with this lovely old lady, I flew back to London to have these two photo sessions of Emperor Hirohito and Golda Meir processed. They were two complete contrasts.

Golda Meir

I was commissioned to cover the visit of Prince Charles and Princess Anne to Canada and the United States of America in 1974. Leaving Canada from Winnipeg I boarded the same aircraft as the royals – it was Air Force One sent by President Nixon. I and three colleagues were given permission to board the flight. The stewards were FBI agents wearing guns on their belts and it was they who served us a sumptuous meal which included lobster. It was a very pleasant flight indeed and we landed at Washington air force base. Of course, we had no formalities on arrival, but when it came to my departure on a special British Airways flight leaving Washington Dallas airport, I had a lot of explaining to do to the airport authorities as to how I landed in America. The aircraft flying Prince Charles back to England had limited passengers and I enjoyed part of the journey with the Prince's aide.

Princess Margaret and Lord Snowdon visited Yugoslavia in 1974. At the end of the visit, I and a colleague Paula James from the *Daily Mirror* had a bet with Princess Margaret and Lord Snowdon that we would arrive first in London by the normal British Airways flight before their royal flight. We arrived over Heathrow and were stacked. Paula went up to our pilot and told him of the bet, asking if he could avoid being stacked. The pilot, somehow or other, managed to persuade ground control, and we landed. But we then had to get over to the north side of the airport where the royal flight would be landing. We got into a taxi – the driver did not want to take us on such a short ride, so we gave him a good tip and we arrived as the royal Andover flight landed. Princess Margaret smiled when she saw us and they both came over and said, "You've won your bet! Now you will come to Kensington Palace for tea."

Several days later I went to the palace. I was sitting with Lord Snowdon in his study when he said to me, "Princess Margaret is in the room next door watching her favourite television programme, Coronation Street, and we will join her later." Several minutes passed when Lord Snowdon said, "I think the programme has now finished, and we will go in for tea now." As we entered a very large lounge I could see the Princess on the telephone in the far corner of the room. She covered the mouthpiece of the telephone, turning round to face me and saying across the room, "Shan't be a moment; I am talking to Mummy."

I thought, 'What a wonderfully natural remark.'

Princess Margaret

The Princess invited me to take photographs of her home in Mustique, aptly named as the island is full of mosquitoes. My wife and I flew from Barbados in a small, light aircraft, and after 45 minutes arrived at the Princess' beautiful villa, Les Jolies Eaux, that overlooked the blue waters of the Caribbean. It was on Mustique that we met Lord Snowdon's uncle, Oliver Messel, who later invited us to his home in Barbados.

In Jamaica for the Commonwealth Games Prince Philip took time off to have a few chukkas at polo. As soon as he saw me, he shouted from his pony, "Why have you come all this way when you can get me at Windsor." He was a good polo player and good to photograph, one must ignore some of his remarks and choice words.

On another occasion I flew to Jamaica and was accredited to *Queen* magazine for the independence of the country. On arrival at Kingston airport a red carpet had been laid to the aircraft's rear entrance, and on departing from the plane I was guided on to the carpet. I was then photographed as I walked along with my camera equipment over my shoulders, laughing and amused, not knowing why I should be the only person walking on the red carpet. When I arrived at the immigration office I asked why was I given such royal treatment; the officer saluted and replied, "Because you are from 'The Queen'." They then gave me a private limousine and chauffer to travel to my residence, which happened to be the local school. At the press meeting I received opposition from colleagues realising that I may obtain better photographic positions and be treated in a different manner as I was listed as 'The Queen'. They shouted out that that I was from *Queen* magazine, not 'The Queen'. There was quite a hullabaloo and my colleagues were obviously very jealous. The officer in charge of the press realised his error and laughed. I then explained that I was representing *Queen* magazine and not Her Majesty, but asked if I could keep the car and driver during my stay. He laughed again and said, "You may have it for 24 hours."

Next was a very long flight to Fiji in the South Pacific. Here the Queen was dressed in a pale pink dress, the temperature above 100 degrees Fahrenheit. I was in a suit, with jacket and tie, and had three cameras over my shoulder and a case. I had to walk with two other cameramen for about a mile to photograph the Queen at a religious ceremony known as the 'Kava Cup.' The Fijian tribesmen gather in a large square, dancing and treading the juices from the roots of a small kawakawa tree. The juice is then offered in a cup to the Queen and Prince Philip to drink. It tasted ghastly – I know, I tasted it.

We – arrived at our photographic positions for the ceremony some 40 feet from the Queen. Unfortunately we were not shaded from the sun and I was overcome by the heat. One of the officials undid my tie and took my cameras off as the straps were cutting my neck, and I was offered a drink. Thankfully it was water and not the juice from the tree. I could see in my camera screen how worried the Queen looked. She was practically ignoring the official ceremony, being more concerned about the safety of one of the three photographers who accompanied her on the tour from England.

Once the ceremony was over, I did not see the Queen for four more days until she arrived at Waitangi – the northern-most tip of New Zealand. I was there on the dockside for her arrival off the royal yacht. When she stepped from the gangway she turned to me and said, "Are you feeling much better now, Mr. Davis?"

I said, "Thank you for enquiring, Ma'am; very much so."

"I am so pleased," Her Majesty said. I mention this story to give you an idea as to how warm, understanding and thoughtful the Queen is.

The Queen and Duke of Edinburgh dancing.

I remember a reception on board Britannia in Auckland. I and three or four of my colleagues were discussing and joking with the Queen when someone dropped a gin and tonic on the deck in front of her. "Don't worry," she said, laughing, and carried on talking as if nothing had happened.

Mexico provided a very colourful state visit in 1975. It was there that the Queen and I tasted 'Daffodil' soup – the obvious name given to a yellow soup. The Mexicans gave the Queen and Prince Philip a fantastic ticker-tape welcome as they were driven through the city. Crowds of girls rushed up to the royal car and threw flowers and bouquets. It was an amazing sight.

On a state visit or an event the 'big' picture occurs in a split second; miss that lightning moment and no king or queen in the world waits for you. On a royal tour lasting perhaps three months, working with your cameras and with half a dozen international magazines and newspapers to supply, you have a great responsibility.

When I covered the wedding of a royal princess in Sweden I wore white tie and tails. I took pictures at the altar in the chapel of the royal castle. I was then escorted through a door behind the altar by one of the King's aides and taken up some stairs to the private apartments where the whole family had assembled for portraits and a family group shot. Afterwards I wanted to pose the bride and groom as they were driving off from the forecourt in an open landau with two footmen behind them on the tail. As I was walking down some steps laden with my equipment, one of my cases was taken from me by Prince Klaus of the Netherlands who said, "Good heavens, man, how can you come dressed like that when you've got all this work to do and so much weight to carry?"

And I said, "Well, I'll tell you. It's very important to be part of the scene, as I have to think about the people I'm photographing more than the pictures I'm taking."

I was invited back to Drottningholm Palace in Stockholm to photograph the new baby, Victoria, with her mother, Queen Silvia. These pictures were taken in one of the lounges and King Carl Gustav and Queen Silvia also posed for me in full regal dress.

The Queen Mother was always caring towards photographers. She would smile, and frequently went out of her way to help them. On one occasion I was particularly grateful for her kindness. Her Majesty was attending a regimental ball at the Hyde Park Hotel in London; I had been commissioned to photograph her with the regimental silver which was on display near the ballroom. Whilst I waited for Her Majesty to review the silver, I had a drink at the bar with the Queen Mother's private secretary. As long as he was there I thought I'd be all right – I never dreamed the Queen Mother might view the silver without telling him. Then a colonel rushed up with the news that Her Majesty had already viewed the silver and was back in the ballroom. The secretary went off to explain what had happened and shortly afterwards he came back to say that Her Majesty would pose especially for me by the silver. I grabbed my equipment and rushed to the display, only to find the Queen Mother had beaten me to it. "Did you enjoy your drink?" she asked me.

Like the Queen, the Queen Mother liked horseracing and enjoyed nothing more than attending Ascot for the Gold Cup. Ascot is a splendid sight to see, with the royal landaus driving down the course in front of the massed crowds in the stand. Together the Queen and Queen Mother would discuss their programme and visit the paddock, then return through the crowds to the royal box to wait for the start of the race. Should they have a winning horse they would go into the unsaddling enclosure to meet the jockey and give the horse a pat. These pictures are very informal and are filed in my library.

The Queen and The Duke of Edinburgh at Ascot.

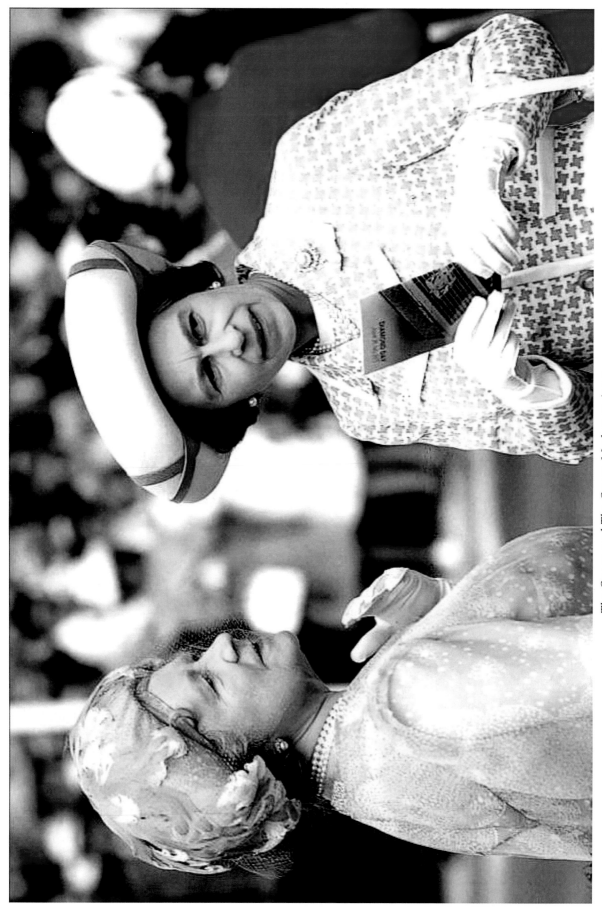

The Queen and The Queen Mother at Ascot.

Princess Sophie of Greece – now Queen of Spain –allowed me to take photographs of her when she was seven months' pregnant, something, surely, that few women would relish, whatever their background. She bathed her other baby and changed the child's napkin. It was simply a fantastic and unusually informal photographic session, as she chatted all the time to me about how to bring up children – a picture session that every magazine editor wishes for, a complete contrast to the formal regalia. When I was in Zarzuela Palace on the outskirts of Madrid I was setting up my equipment in one of the lounges when King Juan Carlos entered dressed in uniform. I thought, 'Oh my God, I've got it all in the wrong position for a formal shot.' I had to rearrange everything rapidly and the King and Queen Sophie helped me move the furniture – a large settee – because I wanted a tapestry in the background. They didn't call any servants; they just pushed furniture around to help me. I liked them very much, but their children – especially the girls, Elena and Christina – tended to squabble and smack each other. Then the Queen turned round and said, "Shut up," like any normal mother. King Juan Carlos sat with me after the session and discussed photography. He is a very keen photographer and talked about cameras, film and taking the children's pictures.

Princess Sophie of Spain and baby Felipe

In 1971 the Shah of Iran arranged a tremendous month-long show across the country to celebrate 2,500 years of the dynasty. At Persepolis, in the heart of the country, the Shah arranged two gala nights. The first one was formal, the second informal. Kings, queens, princes, princesses and heads of state came from all over the world and I was there at the invitation of the Shah. On the second night, the informal one, Prince Philip together with Princess Anne, the President of Turkey and his wife, Marshal Tito of Yugoslavia and his wife were all seated with the Shah. Prince Philip looked at me angrily and called to the Shah, "What's this fellow Davis doing here?" I was dumbstruck. I thought Philip had only to say another word and I'd be thrown out. Only afterwards did my astonishment turn to anger and resentment. The Shah, however, rose magnificently to the occasion and calmly called back, "He's working for me." That shut up Prince Philip, I was pleased to see. The Shah was so pleased with my pictures he gave me a decoration, 'The Order of Taj'. I took a photograph that evening of Princess Anne, her hands cupped to her chin on the table, looking dreamily into the distance, and it won the award for Best Royal Picture of the Year. I was almost as proud of the caption I gave it as I was of the picture – 'A sovereign for your thoughts'.

Princess Anne

Despite what many people think, Princess Anne is somehow special. The private audience she gave me just before her marriage to Captain Mark Phillips, resulted in a superb set of pictures that had global publications – easily the most informal pictures of a British royal ever taken. I was allowed to choose several outfits for her and, with a very informal picture in mind, I asked the ladies-in-waiting if they could add a parasol to the gowns. They didn't have one apparently, but they rushed off to Harrods and obtained one.

Most of the shots were taken beside the lake in the palace grounds. I asked the Princess to lie down in the long grass, as she was wearing a blouse and jeans. I then asked if she would take a piece of straw and put it to her mouth. She said, "I'm not that type of girl." The pictures I took were wonderful, informal and glamourous.

Princess Anne in the high grass

Princess Anne taking a jump

I left my hotel one afternoon, loaded up my cameras and struggled towards a coach that was to take guests of the Shah and myself to the Son et Luminiere performance that night. After a few painful paces ex-King Constantine of Greece came alongside me and said, "You seem to be having a bit of a problem, let me help you carry some." With that he took two heavy cameras from me and lugged them onto the coach.

King Constantine

On another occasion I was photographing Queen Beatrix of Holland in the palace in The Hague. I had to take my equipment from one side of the palace to the other, when I heard a voice say, "That's too much for you to carry." It was the Crown Prince, and he immediately slung half my equipment over his shoulder and carried it for me.

My wife and I always confer a night before a session and go through ideas for informal pictures. It was her idea, since Holland is known for cyclists, to ask the Queen if she would ride a bicycle. Having taken lots of shots of the Queen and her family, I asked the Queen if there was a bicycle available for her to ride for a picture. She went away and returned with a tandem and insisted that her husband Prince Klaus take the front seat. I actually took 12 pictures of them cycling in the garden. Unfortunately only one was approved for distribution; the other 11 were killed. My wife has a keen eye for these things and said, "It's probably because she didn't like the view of her rear." Still, I am pleased to say that the one surviving picture published all over the world.

Queen Beatrix of The Netherlands and Prince Klaus cycling

Queen Beatrix and Prince Klaus have three sons, all of whom wanted to carry my camera equipment. For the first picture I took, I posed the boys around the head of their mother who was seated on the lawn. I called the picture *My Three Sons*. It was just four heads together and they were all full of life. The reason for their joy was because I asked their father to sit with me and he did some tricks that made them laugh. I took shots of them on the edge of a lake where one could see white and even a black swan floating around. I also photographed them leaning over a small bridge. The session lasted two and a half hours. It was a lovely family gathering.

Queen Beatrix and her three sons

I had arranged exclusively to photograph the Dutch Royal Family on their skiing holiday in Lech, Austria. My hotel was up a mountain side and the paths were icy and dangerous. I was so petrified of falling with my valuable photographic equipment that I bought myself a pair of heavy leather boots, but I forgot to get some thick woolly socks to wear with them. The result was that I kept getting sharp shooting pains up the back of my legs until I discovered, back at my hotel, that the backs of my ankles were caked in blood where the boots had cut into my skin. The welts took over a month to heal.

A fun royal was Princess Georgina of Liechtenstein. After I had photographed her with her husband in the palace at Vaduz, the capital of the principality, I told her I was going back to London on the train. "Oh, you'll need something to eat on the journey," she said. She disappeared for a few minutes and came back with a big bag of apples. The apples were sweet and red and I ate some on the way home.

I flew to Oslo to photograph the young royal couple, Prince Harald and Miss Sonja Haraldsen, for their engagement. (They are now King and Queen.) When I arrived at the Royal Palace they seemed a little nervous. It was my first meeting with them and I could understand why they were tense. Many people hate being photographed and a photographic session, particularly with a stranger, can be an ordeal. The evening was spent taking formal pictures in full dress. The following morning was bright and sunny, perfect for some informal shots outside in the grounds. I wanted to try and get a tender loving pose, so I asked Sonja if she would perhaps lean against a tree and if Prince Harald could lean next to her shoulder and hold her hand. The prince hesitated and I could see he wasn't too happy about my idea, but somehow or other he accepted. They looked at each other, smiling, as she held his hand which was round her shoulder. I got my loving picture. Sonja was wearing a pale green suit, Prince Harald was in loungewear. When I had finished taking, Prince Harald noticed the back of Sonja's jacket was full of dust. He duly brushed it off, and as I said goodbye he turned to me and said jokingly, "Next time you come to Norway, Mr. Davis, remind me to get the trees washed for you." We all laughed.

Prince Harald of Norway and Miss Sonja Haraldsen

I have often been asked who the most difficult royal I've ever photographed was. Without doubt, it was Princess Grace of Monaco. "You can have a private audience with me only if you have had a private photographic audience with the Queen of England." she said. It left me in no doubt about the level at which she rated herself. Nonetheless, I did later have an exclusive audience in the Prince's Palace of Monaco. At the audience I asked Princess Grace if she would play the piano, with Prince Rainier and the children gathered round her, as it would make a good picture. "I don't play the piano," she said sulkily.

"Well, could you just sit by the piano while I take a family shot?" She finally agreed, lifted the lid of the piano, then began to play like a concert pianist.

'What was all that about?' I asked myself wearily. Haughty, arrogant, distant beyond belief – that was Miss Grace Kelly when she got her tin-pot royal handle. She certainly wasn't the sort of person you'd dare remind that her old granddad was an Irish bricklayer, not for all the chips in the Monte Carlo casino.

Princess Grace of Monaco

I have had so many royal audiences that I can remember all over the world, but when these pictures were published there was a great deal of resentment and jealousy. I was bitterly attacked by the Swedish and Dutch press because an Englishman was given the privilege of having exclusive audiences photographing their royal family, and it was said, "Why is this foreigner being given privileged facilities to photograph our royals?" The Swedish press called me "a playboy who rides around the world in his Rolls Royce." My car not only impressed the local press but it also impressed the Grand Duke of Luxembourg. He drove it round the palace grounds and on returning he said," It handles beautifully and so smooth, I may buy one," he told me.

Princess Grace playing the piano

It's always fun with the Prince of Wales when he's alone. At the Badminton horse trials in 1976 he emerged sporting a beard and seemed very pleased with himself. Having gone to bed late, I didn't arrive until 11am. Charles called out, "Hello Reg, haven't seen you anywhere this morning. I thought you decided to stay in bed all day." Guessing he wanted me to take a picture of the beard, I replied cheerily, "No sir, I am here and ready to start work." The publication of the beard picture was a hit.

Prince Charles with beard.

In Nassau at the Bahamas Independence Day celebration it was very hot and I decided to spend a lunch break sunning myself on the beach. That was a mistake, for my legs became badly sunburned and all afternoon I was hobbling around in pain. That evening there was a ball and the Prince, dancing a calypso, called to me to come and join in. "I'm afraid I can't, sir," I moaned. "My legs are sunburned and I'm in pain." The next day he came to see me in my hotel room. "I'm sorry you got burned yesterday," he said. "I hope you're not suffering. If there is anything we can do for you, just give us a shout."

Prince Charles in a helicopter.

A few hours later I was to see a very different Prince of Wales. He had gone along to the polo club for a couple of chukkas and a large crowd was watching. There was a commentary on the game over the loud speaker by a commentator who, I'm sorry to say, needed his head examined. "There goes Charlie with his stick in the air," he roared from the microphone. "He takes a swipe at it and misses. That's Charlie, the Queen's son. Never mind, Charlie boy, some you hit, some you miss." At the end of the chukka the Prince dismounted – and all could see by the fixed expression on his face exactly what was going to happen next. He passed his pony to his groom and strode purposefully towards the commentary box. What was said inside can't be repeated in a respectable publication but it was the talk of Nassau for days afterwards. I'm fairly certain, too, that it was the last commentary that commentator ever made in the Bahamas.

Prince Charles at polo.

Not all of my work is devoted to the world's royalty. Informal photographs of personalities in the public eye are also much in demand by editors. One of the top women outside royalty who could command an editor's immediate attention was Jacqueline Kennedy. I had photographed her on three occasions. Once in London, in Seville in Spain, and on her Acapulco holiday in Mexico. She was always charming and cooperative, but in Acapulco the Mexican authorities decided to intervene. "There will be no pictures," they ruled of their own volition. I had travelled a long way for this photographic assignment. So I hired a motor boat and driver and put to sea to photograph the holidaying Kennedys in their dinghy. The Mexican authorities had anticipated this manoeuvre and within a very short time a gunboat was bearing down on my frail craft on collision course. It hit my boat on the stern quarter and rocked it perilously. Somehow, though, we managed to keep afloat – luckily for me and my cameras. I need hardly add that these are not the best conditions in which to take photographs. Twice more the gunboat rammed my boat and still she kept upright. Then, disaster! As the gunboat swung round for another go, its wake caused the Kennedy's dinghy to capsize and the Kennedy family – Jackie and her two children – were thrown into the water. There, before my eyes, was the news picture story of the year and I made the best of the opportunity. The resultant pictures of the Kennedys' ducking caused no harm and the situation was treated as a huge joke by Mrs. Kennedy.

Jackie Kennedy in dinghy.

1976 was America's bicentennial year and the year the Queen paid a state visit to the United States of America. Prior to the visit I had an exclusive photo session with Elizabeth Taylor which was held in an apartment on 5th Avenue. I had met Elizabeth a few days before in her hotel and, believe it or not, our talk was held in her bedroom, sitting on the edge of the bed. 'Very intimate,' I thought at the time. The photo session lasted roughly two hours and, in between changing her clothes, she would go into an adjoining room and have a glass of champagne. She would bring the bottle into the room where I was setting up my equipment for the next position. During the session she asked me, "Could you arrange for me to go on board the Royal Yacht?"

"That would be impossible," I said. "However, I could possibly arrange for you to be at the cocktail evening at the British Embassy in Washington."

"I need a partner; could you escort me?" she asked. I told her that would be impossible as I would be photographing at that time but that I would speak to someone at the Iranian Embassy and arrange a suitable escort for her. The session over, she threw her arms around me, gave me a hug, kissed me on both cheeks and left. Later I was able to make the necessary arrangements for her. I knew a Mr. John Warner who I had previously met at the Iranian Embassy and who readily agreed to be her escort. I photographed them meeting the Queen on their arrival and later that year they married.

Elizabeth Taylor

The pictures I took of Elizabeth were great but they had to go to her for approval before being published. It was arranged to meet her in the Imperial Hotel in Vienna, as she would be in Europe during the later part of the year. I decided to have a chaperone with me as I did not have too much trust in Elizabeth. I took with me an Italian colleague, Gabrielle Pantucci. We arrived at the hotel and were shown up to her room. She seemed to be well over the limit and we could see an open bottle of Jack Daniels whisky on the table. Elizabeth asked how I was. She then started to look at the transparent film of the images by holding each image up to her eyes and either giving it to me or placing it on the table in front of her. She more or less said, "One for you and one for me." With that, we left Vienna with half of the material approved. I was not very happy with the situation but had no option but to accept.

Elizabeth Taylor

One of the most beautiful women I had recently photographed was Princess Paola of Belgium. She is now Queen. I photographed her in her residence Le Chateau de Belvedere in Brussels, which is set in immaculately kept grounds. She met me in a smart cerise afternoon dress. "Hallo, Mr. Davis, now I'd like you to tell me exactly what you want me to do," she said. We walked into the nursery. It was a large, brightly decorated room and the whole of one wall was covered with whitewood shelves crammed with soft toys and dolls. Scattered round were even more toys, a doll's table, animals and toys on wheels. Her three golden-haired children were sitting in the centre of the room on small wicker chairs, playing with bricks. Princess Paola tried to coax them, "Come on, children, let me help you with your bricks." I took all my shots in the nursery, then the Princess suggested that I should photograph the children riding their bikes outside. They cycled happily for me, racing around on the sandstone pathway. Afterwards we went back to the chateau for tea.

Later I photographed Princess Paola sitting framed in the doorway of the garden summerhouse with the background of the chateau. Then she posed for me in blue jeans and a yellow blouse, reclining against a tree, and later in the high grass, her golden hair flowing in the gentle breeze. I left the chateau very excited, knowing I had some lovely shots.

I was asked to go to the Belgian Embassy in London to show the Princess the pictures. I arrived early one morning and was told the princess was not yet available. A few minutes later I was informed she was now ready to receive me and that the butler would take me up to her bedroom. I walked up the gilt staircase feeling apprehensive. The butler knocked at her door on the landing and a moment later Princess Paola popped her head round the door.

Princess Paola of Belgium

She wore a blue satin dressing gown, her long blonde hair flowing loosely around her shoulders and she had no make-up on. She had obviously just arisen. "Please forgive me, I don't feel very well today," she told me. In the early hours of the morning light and without make-up, her beauty was stunning. She looked through the pictures and seemed very happy. She thanked me. With that I left with the photographs to be released – they were fabulous. I could see the similarity of her to the film actress, Joan Fontaine.

She is without doubt one of the most beautiful women in the world and certainly one of the most photogenic. The petite softly-spoken Italian-born Princess has large expressive green eyes and is a frequent trendsetter in hairstyles. Her perfect features make her an ideal subject for a photographer. When she makes a public appearance I never fail to see spectators elbow each other and hear the whisper, "Isn't she lovely."

It was my fourth exclusive audience with the beautiful Princess – two had been in London and this, my second visit, was to her home in Brussels, Le Chateau de Belvedere, situated on the outskirts of Brussels to the north of the city on the road to Antwerp. It is set in beautiful grounds with long, wide carriage drives, reminiscent, I thought, of my first visit to Versailles. I entered a large entrance hall in which many doors opened. It had an attractive staircase on the right, and a floor of black and white marble squares. I was shown up the staircase and into a large lounge, and left alone to set up my cameras. One of the aides entered and informed me, "The Princess will not be too long." There were many royal photographs in black and white displayed on the shelves and tables, most of them signed. They included pictures of King Feisal of Saudi Arabia, Grand Duke Jean of Luxembourg and his family, Queen Elizabeth and Prince Philip, the Shah of Iran, Juan Carlos of Spain and one of King Constantine of Greece.

I decided, after having set up my cameras, to wander through to another lounge which led to a terrace and the garden. Several minutes passed before the Princess arrived dressed in a pair of denim trousers and an open-necked matching shirt with white spots. She said, "How nice it is to see you again after so long. I thought your book, *Royalty of the World*, was very good and, I must say, you certainly have had a great deal of variety in the countries you visited over the years in making it. Are you going to make another?" I told her my plans for making a book on 'royal families of the world'. The Princess told me she liked people who are artistic. "I have a lot of time for them, they put so much effort into their achievements."

Willingly, the Princess changed clothes several times. She asked what I would like and where she should stand. "Perhaps you will take the children tomorrow," she said. With the audience over, we sat on the terrace over cool drinks and chatted about many things. "I must show you the family album," she said, and with that she left me sipping my drink. On returning several minutes later, she had changed her clothes yet again. We sat down and she set the album on our knees. "These are some of my favourites," she said, showing me several pages.

She told me her holidays were spent on the ski resorts of Switzerland in the winter and in Sardinia in the summer, and Rome and Milan during – in the autumn. Turin in northern Italy is where her family, the Gazzellis, live; it's her spiritual home. The marriage of Paola and Albert is a very happy one. "The attraction of the opposites make harmony," she said. There are three children from the marriage – Philippe, Astrid and Laurant.

Princess Paola shops at Jean Louis Scherrer's very exclusive and expensive house in Paris and at Pina Vacchetta in Turin. The latter made her wedding gown.

Photographing the Luxembourg royal family was a delight; they were a perfectly natural family. I lunched with the Grand Duke, Grand Duchess and one of their sons, and the Grand Duke served from the buffet. It was so normal, like being at home. The Grand Duke was very interested in my car, which was a Rolls-Royce Silver Spirit. He said he had never driven one, and then enquired, "Can I drive yours after lunch."

"Certainly," I replied. And so he did. He drove it in the grounds of the palace and returned with a smile, "It handles so smoothly."

The Princess Maria Teresa was so excited with the photographs I had taken of her, both formal and informal, that she decided to fly to London to my home and see the finished results. She arrived on a sunny morning and smiled as my wife and I welcomed her. She viewed the photographs and was extremely pleased. We sat down for lunch with my wife and daughter and had a very pleasant time. Later she left to catch her plane home.

Grand Duchess Marie Teresa of Luxembourg

The first of the photographic settings was in the tiered garden of her home – in Fischbach Castle – and was set in an archway on the third level of the grounds. Crown Prince Henri was wearing a pale cream cardigan and his wife a similar colour. She turned and said to him, "Henri, why don't you go and change into a different colour sweater?" With that he turned, went up three levels of the gardens and returned wearing a red cardigan. "Absolutely perfect," Maria Teresa said. After the session my wife and I were invited to lunch. We sat together like any normal family and had a very enjoyable meal.

I was then invited to the home of Princess Marie Astrid, in Geneva, and it was there that I was given lunch that had been specially prepared by the Princess. "I won't let you take any photographs until you have eaten," she said. With that, she sat with me and talked as I ate. Sweet, charming Princess Marie Astrid sipped apple juice through a straw and told me about her married life with His Imperial Highness Archduke Christian of Austria – while I ate my lunch. "We have an absolutely marvellous time here in Geneva," she said. "My parents visit us as often as possible, and we make return visits to them as often as we can. My husband and I have lunch in the city when he's free and we use the time to share all our experiences, joking and laughing about the funny things that are always happening to us."

"My wife has a tremendous sense of humour," Prince Christian told me. "She makes me laugh a lot."

I asked her, had she not been born a princess what career would she have chosen. I was prepared for the answer. "A doctor," she said. "You see, I love nursing." Archduke Christian nodded. "She is a very caring person," he said. "Her position as a princess at least gives her an opportunity to fulfil a caring role. I want to tell you that she is a very good cook and her love of cooking Chinese meals is a reflection of her frequent visits to the Far East. And her cheese soufflés are simply spectacular!" enthused Prince Christian. For me, however, it was neither a Chinese nor a soufflé occasion. My lunch that day, served by Princess Marie Astrid herself, was meat, peas and mashed potatoes.

The soaring of the castle was incised on the skyline above a thick belt of trees, etched in a distant frame of early-morning mist that made it, at once, enchantingly magic and curiously inaccessible. I could see the castle. The problem was, how to get there. I stopped my car on the country road. As the King says in *The King and I*, it was "a puzzlement" At that moment a window of a country cottage at the roadside was thrown open and an old, gap-toothed large-bosomed Luxembourgeoise appeared, framed in its open rectangle. She eyed me suspiciously, for it was still only 7am. For an answer, the old woman shook her head emphatically, threw her arms open wide and slammed the window shut.

'Was the distant castle really enchanted?' I wondered, 'And was this the wicked witch? Or, much more probably, was my French accent as incomprehensible for the natives of this unusual little country as it sometimes is even to the French themselves?' I say 'unusual' because there are still many Europeans who wouldn't quite be able to place Luxembourg on a map of their continent and who wouldn't be quite certain whether it enjoyed the status of a principality, dukedom, kingdom or republic, and who wouldn't be quite sure whether it had a language of its own or a language borrowed from a neighbour. I will set the record straight: Luxembourg is a Grand Duchy. "We are regarded in Europe as a rich country," the Grand Duke told me.

The Grand Duke is a competent skier and water skier. He also likes hunting and fishing. Away from the sports field his next love is music. "I like Mozart and Haydn and the earlier composers like Telemann, Vivaldi and Corelli. On the whole, I prefer orchestral compositions and I especially like going to concerts whenever time permits. I also have a lot of folk music recordings from all over the world, which I love listening to.

Princess Maria Teresa, now the Grand Duchess of Luxembourg, was born in Havana, Cuba. She told me, "I always feel warm towards the Luxembourg people because they are always so kind to me. From the moment I arrived here they made me feel at home very quickly." The Grand Duchess's husband is Grand Duke Henri. She told me, "At weekends when we are together we simply do everything on our own. My husband and I both cook, and he cooks as often as I do. I usually do meat and rice dishes, and sauces to go with spaghetti. My husband likes doing steaks and he particularly likes barbeques. I think we are a very close couple and that's what our friends always say."

The Princess told me that she thought the change in her life from being a single woman to a married woman with three children was probably a bigger emotional difference to adjust to than the difference in her life caused by marrying into a royal family. "Royal protocol and the obvious constraints of being of royal blood has really never burdened me," she said. "I suppose that's because I'm very much in love, and that, in itself, made the transition easy. In that sense life has been very good to me. I never hesitate to call my mother-in-law for help," she said. "Her advice is always precious."

When I photographed Princess Margaretha of Liechtenstein, a daughter of The Grand Duke and Grand Duchess of Luxembourg, she was in the middle of moving from her Strasbourg flat to a house in Berne, where her husband Prince Nikolaus of Liechtenstein had just been appointed his country's ambassador to Switzerland. "Well, it certainly has given me a first-hand insight into the problems people have sometimes to put up with living in a flat," she told me when I asked her if she was relieved to be moving to a comfortable Swiss house, complete with its own spacious garden. "Like, for instance, not knocking nails into the walls after 10 o'clock at night so as not to disturb the neighbours, the noise, the lack of a private garden, having always to take the children to a public park to play, and watch over them so that they didn't get into any unhygienic situations. These were also some drawbacks. Still, it undoubtedly did wonderful things for developing the social side of my character because I've always been a bit shy."

"You know, it is an astonishing thing to give birth to another human being," the Princess told me. "It never ceases to fill me with wonder. Being a princess, the most important thing for me, therefore, is always to represent a certain standard of moral and ethical values. There are 22 embassies in Strasbourg, so we got to know each other rather well." she said. "In Berne there are more than 70, so we shall have lots of new people to meet." Princess Margaretha is an enthusiastic sportswoman. Swimming, skiing and water skiing are favourites, and she particularly loves jogging. "I also like listening to music, both modern and classical. My favourite composers are Vivaldi and Mendelssohn. I love going to concerts and musicals."

Sophia Loren, the vibrant, vivacious woman who I first photographed in 1975 was as captivating and exotic as ever. The enthusiasm and sparkle of this stunningly beautiful woman was as regal as any queen or princess it has been my privilege to have photographed. I was invited to photograph her at her luxury home in Paris.

I decided that she was a perfect subject for a tiara. Sophia, who was giving me a break from royal audiences, readily agreed to this regal touch. But where, I wondered, could I find a tiara in a republic which had long ago abandoned royalty. Sophia at once provided the answer. "I'll ring Dior's," she said. "They will help with the gowns and Gerrard's will help with some jewels." An hour later I was negotiating the several-million-pound arrangement and giving my instructions for the delivery of a gem-studded tiara.

It was here in Paris that I first met Gerrard the Jeweller in the Avenue Montaigne, and I said to him, "I don't like these at all," handing him back a two-million-pound diamond necklace. "I don't think they would look right on Miss Sophia Loren."

"How about these, sir?" the jeweller ventured, presenting me with four million pounds worth of diamonds and rubies. "We will make them up into a tiara overnight, if you like."

"They're better," I said. "They are elegant; they would be ideal." My amazing diamond experience at Gerrard's was no Walter Mitty fantasy.

The next day, as it is my custom, I arrived early at the location – Sophia's three-floor apartment in the heart of the city – to set up my cameras and check the background, lighting and other equipment. She came into the room. She was stunningly beautiful, as regal as any of the great queens and princesses I have photographed, and a perfect model for the four million pounds worth of sparkling gems I had borrowed from Gerrard's. She was wearing a lemon gown covered in a yellow ostrich-feathered bolero. "Surely you don't work with your jacket on?" she asked at once. "Why don't you take it off and make yourself at home." All that day Sophia talked and joked while I worked. Effortlessly, she slipped from Dior evening creations and the millions of pounds of jewels into blue jeans and a blouse, and back into Dior gowns again, looking amazingly perfect for each outfit. All the time she chatted vivaciously until I was quite sure that I had never met anyone with so much enthusiasm and so much sparkle.

Sophia Loren

On the second day of my session Sophia's husband, the Italian film producer Carlo Ponti, was in the apartment. At 7am that day he had arrived back from a film business trip to New York. He had rested briefly, then, at Sophia's request, he had come to join the session in the main drawing room. His entrance was almost as dramatic as hers had been the previous day. As soon as he entered the doorway Sophia leapt up from the settee where I had posed her, threw her arms around him and began kissing him affectionately.

Discreetly, I turned and gazed out at the tide of people in the unsleeping Avenue George V "Did you take a photograph of us?" Sophia called out. 'Of course not', "But why not? Now, take a photograph of us!" Lovingly she kissed him again and I, having thus temporarily lost command of giving the photographic instructions, dutifully complied with her request.

Sophia told me that she had had her hair specially done for the photographic session by Alexandre of Faubourg Saint-Honoré, coiffeur to the top stars. During the session she added a new dimension to Dior's elegant new furs and gowns by trying some of the new hats by Jean Barthet. But it was the exquisite jewels that commanded so much attention when displayed by my splendid model. I remember the magnificent gems worn by Empress Farah when I photographed her in Iran and the gorgeous diamond tiara worn by Her Majesty Queen Elizabeth at the State Opening of Parliament. All those priceless jewels were outshone by the Gerard collection, in which Sophia Loren posed for my photographs. Among them was a tiara of pure diamonds, two fabulous rubies of 25 carats each, a collection of pear-shaped diamonds with a pear on the necklace of 38 carats, a pair of 80-carat sapphire earrings and a 35-carat ruby ring from Burma.

Sophia Loren and her husband Carlo Ponti

I asked Sophia about the disappointments she had felt in her life. She told me that one of the greatest sorrows she had experienced was the loss of her Italian citizenship. This had been forced upon her in the early 1960s, so that she could be free to marry Carlo Ponti, the man she loved. He too had to renounce his citizenship since, having been married previously, his divorce was not recognised by Italian law at that time. Throughout my two-day session I was full of admiration for her resilience in front of the cameras. I asked her if she liked being photographed. "Yes, but only by photographers whom I like. I find you easy to work with." Then she added, laughing, "But you tend to devote as much attention to the creative side of your work as if it were your own child. You shouldn't worry so much, it isn't good for you."

Years later another session took place in one of the most picturesque cities in the world – Rome – a setting just perfect for such a woman. It was here in the Piazza Farnese, at the Embassy of France in Italy that I photographed the Queen of the screen, Sophia. The gowns came from Azzaro, Louis Scherrer and Valentino. "I adore red," she told me. To enhance the gown I chose a simple background in the garden of climbing ivy, with subdued sunlight and a plain white stone garden seat; and she loved it. The jewellery which was carefully selected from Bulgari on the Via Condotti. Her hair was styled by Giovanni D'Arpa. Victoria de Sica once described her as "a revelation", and Clark Gable once said of her, "All that meat on the bone and every ounce of it a choice enough to eat."

"Arriverderci" Sophia said, then stepping forward she kissed me on both cheeks. I left with the feeling that the lovely Sophia is not only a great star, but she is also a lovely human being.

Sophia Loren

I raised my camera in front of the beautiful Queen Sirikit at the royal palace at Chiang Mai in Thailand, and moved my finger on to the shutter release. I had flown approximately 6,000 miles to take this royal feature; nothing must be allowed to spoil it. I felt my metabolism becoming screwed up – the kind of 'inside ache' a golfer must have when the championship prize hangs on the outcome of a short putt. Suddenly the hot humid silence was broken, with an almost continuous clicking sound from somewhere behind me. The tension snapped. With a photographer's instinct I recognised that sound instantly. Someone with a camera was calmly muscling in on the regal pose I had set up with such care. Irritably, I swung round to challenge the intruder, and there, standing right behind me and calmly clicking his camera, was His Majesty King Bhumibol Adulyadej of Thailand, husband of Queen Sirikit.

The King, a keen amateur photographer, was apparently so interested in the pose I had arranged for his magnificent wife that he decided to shoot it himself. I can laugh at that moment now, but when that incident happened on my royal assignment in Thailand I had to pass through the emotions of annoyance, astonishment and apology in a split second. Hastily I stepped back to give the photographer King a clear field of vision. "I'm so sorry, sir," I said. "If you would like to continue, I will gladly wait for you."

"No, please carry on," the King replied, while our delightful model continued to smile that light endearing smile that is the universal attribute of the ladies of Thailand. Then I had an inspiration, "Would you like to take a picture with this camera, sir?" I said, offering the King one of my cameras. "I will get it for you." A moment later the King had used my camera to take a picture of his wife, and this time I was behind him taking a picture of the King taking a picture. This was just one of the amusing incidents that happened on the assignment that took me on a 12-hour jet flight from London to the fairy-tale summer palace of the King and Queen of Thailand.

Intrigued by the beauty of this eastern Queen and mother of a prince and three princesses, I had requested and received permission from Her Majesty to spend two days with the royal family at Bhuping Palace in Chiang Mai. This was their holiday home, five hundred miles north of Bangkok, the capital of Thailand. My plane flew from an England suffering in a low temperature to a Thailand sweltering in the nineties. Waiting for me at the airport was an official of the royal household. Over an excellent traditional Thai dinner he briefed me for the flight for the following day. The flight was a bus stop one, stopping every 30 miles, and I lost count of the times we came down and took off again from all the local airports en-route. The city of Chiang Mai is 100 miles from the Burmese border and Bhuping Palace is just 11 miles outside the city. How did I counter the mounting nervous tension? I was driven in the royal car from the airport and I counted 194 bends in the road overhanging 64 sheer precipices.

Bhuping Palace is a magnificent sight when approached from any angle. The kings and queens of Denmark, Belgium and Holland, and the German president were guests here during their state visits to Thailand. The palace is set in superbly laid out ornamental gardens that reminded me of a huge Chinese pagoda. The officials however assured me that it was typical Thai-style architecture, quite different from the Chinese. And then I had a surprise! In the lounge of the royal palace to where I had been conducted, an official touched my elbow "Mr Davis," he said, "allow me to introduce to you Anna of Siam!"

Queen Sirikit of Thailand

79

"Hello," said a warm Scottish voice. "How nice to meet an Englishman after all this time. I'm Maureen Gordon from Aberdeen and I'm here to help the Crown Prince and the Princesses improve their English and to teach them English ways." I was flabbergasted to meet this tall fair Scotswoman, genuinely and jocularly referred to as 'Anna of Siam' by the officials. At the age of 29, Maureen had been recommended by the British Council in London for her exciting job and had arrived in January this year. "Well, I must be off," said Maureen cheerfully, "It's nearly time for lessons." In that moment I was asked to wait in the lounge and to look around the spacious drawing room where it was suggested I set up my cameras.

The magnificent black marble flooring was set off with a deeply piled red carpet. One end of the room was entirely glass and beyond was a gaily coloured terrace overlooking a sunken tea pavilion. A court official had warned me to look out for the approach of the King and Queen through a door in the corner of the vast room. I had not long to wait. It was no sooner had I set my cameras that I looked up to see the entire royal family coming through the door. The King and Queen, the 11-year-old Crown Prince Vajiralongkorn and the three princesses – ten-year-old Ubol Ratana, nine-year-old Sirindhorn and six-year-old Chulabhorn.

How can I describe the astonishing beauty of Queen Sirikit? No matter where she is in the room, one is immediately aware of being in the presence of incomparable and enchanting loveliness. She is petite, raven-haired with a warm-toned pearly skin and has quite the best complexion I have ever seen. When she smiles, which is often, she shows even glittering white teeth and her smile is like warm hospitality. They came towards me with the King holding the hand of one of the little princesses. I heard a court official murmur, "Mr Davis," then I bowed and shook hands with the King and his charming Queen.

The Queen, on the first of my two-day photographic session, wore a brilliant orange silk jacket and a long multi-coloured skirt – the traditional northern Thai style dress – her hair in Edwardian fashion. The princesses were in European dresses, all in yellow. The King suggested I should first take a formal group. It proved the most difficult of all, for every time I was about to take the picture the six-year-old Princess Chulabhorn – whose name means 'supreme beauty,' – turned her back on me. "I am sorry," the King said. "She doesn't like the flash." Then in Thai, he and the Queen apparently appeared to reason with the Princess. It was at this stage (I learned afterwards) that the King commented to an official, "Mr Davis is going to have a hard time. I feel quite sorry for him."

Seconds later I was beginning to feel sorry for myself. With the royal group nicely and precisely arranged, and my hand poised to release the shutter, the electrical contacts on my flash failed. "I am sorry," I said, "I do apologise." The King shrugged sympathetically and the children roared with laughter.

Back inside the drawing room Queen Sirikit agreed to pose for me on a long gilded settee with a triangular silk cushion at the head. We talked the whole time, the Queen speaking in a soft mellow tone and annunciating slowly and distinctly. I asked her if she had any particular hobbies. "I love the piano," she answered me, smiling. "I also do Swedish exercises, a sort of gymnastic rhythm to music. It helps me to keep me in form and in good health. I do these exercises every morning. I also love travelling and I think it is a great advantage to be able to get to know the world. I am fond of England. – My favourite cities are San Francisco, Lausanne and Hamburg. I am always busy, I am President of the Thai Red Cross and am patron of the Blind Association."

"Have you ever thought, if you were not the Queen, what you would do?" I asked.

"I would like to be a concert pianist," she replied without hesitation, or, failing that, a piano teacher. You see, I love the piano very much."

"I am a great admirer of your Queen Elizabeth," she told me. "I like the English very much. I do not say that because you come from England, but I really mean it. The English are a very sporting people and they are very good friends to have. They are also charming to their foreign visitors. I am also very fond of the Australians – they seem to be very well off and very happy. I love to go walking, hiking and camping when we are out of the capital," she said. "I am deeply interested in my children's education. I would like my son to study abroad but have not yet decided where. I would want the girls to finish all their education in Thailand, then they can go abroad afterwards."

The court officials, always kind and co-operative, now offered me tea and fruit, and a scotch and soda, to end the day.

When I arrived at the palace the next day, the King and his mother were seated at a table and framing pressed flowers in books for a collection they were keeping. I took photographs of them as they studied intensely, after which I walked out onto the terrace. It was already very hot and humid, and as I looked across the breathtaking view of the valley I was reminded of Switzerland. Then the Queen came towards me, wearing a lemon coloured Balmain dress of Jersey silk. Her black glossy hair falling on her shoulders shone in the strong sunlight. We shook hands and even in the intense heat she was a willing and helpful model. Once again I heard the persistent clicking sound of the camera behind me. It was the King who seemed to like the poses I had selected for his charming wife. We went inside to the drawing room and I noticed a piano there. I asked the Queen if she would play for me. She sat on the stool and started playing; I immediately recognised the tune. It was Jingle Bells, and it was being sung by the Queen and the children.

By lunchtime my assignment was finished, and as I strolled across the terrace with Queen Sirikit towards the waiting King, she apologised for not having any royal regalia in the palace. "We are here for a month," she explained, "and I haven't even brought a small tiara with me, but you must come to Thailand again Mr. Davis and take some pictures of us in the royal palaces at Bangkok."

I bowed, shook hands and left one of the most charming royal families it has ever been my privilege to photograph.

When I returned to Bangkok two years later, Thailand was still the same sun-baked old-world country, but it had also become the centre of a politically explosive sub-continent. For the very first time I began to understand the unique esteem in which the Thai people hold their monarchy – and the unique esteem in which the Thai monarchy hold their people. For, said Queen Sirikit in reply to my frank inquiry: "When you ask about the political situation in this part of the world I am very pleased to give you an answer. If a political change in Thailand forced my husband, the King, and I to leave the country we would not know where to go. We have never elected for any one country where we might go into exile, for the simple reason that we have enough faith in our country and our people never to have given the matter a thought. We love our people, and their unity is our unity."

This time Their Majesties were in residence in Bangkok, that exotic riverine city. When we discussed politics the Queen recalled more peaceful times. "Life has changed a great deal for me," she said. "I used to dance and sing and have a good time, but now I have to shoulder my responsibilities. My husband, you know, is a serious-minded man and very conscientious about his duties towards his people and the country." I have photographed royal families all over the world and never have I met such a deep-rooted sense of public duty as I have seen in the Thai royal family. Time and time again, that conscientiousness of responsibility and even accountability punctuated the conversations during the audiences I was given. That this affection for the people is eagerly reciprocated was amply demonstrated when I spoke at random to men and women in the street of Bangkok. On telling them that I was in Thailand to photograph their Majesties, one man said, "My Queen is beautiful.

She loves everyone and she is kind to the poor."

A waiter said simply, "For me, my Queen is the first lady in the world because I love her."

And a shopkeeper told me, "She is so beautiful. She helps so many poor people and she is so intelligent. They are altogether a wonderful family."

Queen Sirikit's dark eyes moistened when I told her about these unsolicited tributes. "My friends have told me of similar experiences they have had when talking with me," she said softly. "I think I have always done my best to help them whenever I could." Once when I was photographing the Queen the temperature began to creep up into the hundreds. The suit I was wearing had been dry-cleaned four times in four days. "Why don't you take your jacket off?" the Queen suggested. Another day the ladies-in-waiting fanned Queen Sirikit as I took pictures of her, but, unluckily for me, not a breath of air from the fans came my way.

During a royal banquet given in my honour at the Grand Palace in Bangkok, the King and I talked about many interests – photography, philosophy and keeping fit. "I don't really like my wife being photographed," he confided. "I'm very jealous of photographers because I like taking pictures of the Queen myself. I never throw away any pictures I have taken of her, even if they are ones that I don't particularly like. You know, Her Majesty photographs best without make-up. Another of my pet dislikes is making speeches. Once, when I was in America I gave a speech that lasted only 20 minutes, after the previous speaker had addressed the audience for two hours. I am sure they expected more from me, but they were kind enough afterwards to come and shake my hand and congratulate me. History is not one of my favourite subjects; I don't like it at all and I have no ambitions to be a great king and go down in history. When great kings reign, Mr. Davis, there are invariably wars during their lifetime, I want my people to be happy and free of war during my reign."

On one occasion I took my wife to Thailand and introduced her to the Queen's private secretary who took a liking to her. She arranged a private viewing of the Grand Palace and the private apartments. Later my wife and I were told to be ready the following day, as we would be going on the royal barge to the old capital. It was truly amazing as the boat slowly wove its way up-river; boats along the way blew their whistles and hooted to cheer us. The ride was two hours and we took a fantastic picnic lunch en-route. On landing from the boat we were met by cars for our drive back to Bangkok. As we drove through the villages the crowds cheered us, and we, in turn, waved our appreciation to the people.

Later that day I was photographing the King and Queen in the throne room of the Grand Palace in Bangkok. Our flight home was due to leave Bangkok that evening, returning to London. I left my wife at the hotel and arranged for her to have a car to the airport. I said I would meet her there after I had finished photographing Their Majesties. As I was taking the photographs I was looking at my watch. Seeing the time going quickly, I realised that I would be late for my flight. I mentioned my predicament to the secretary and said that I was worried about missing the flight. She said, "Mr. Davis, please do not worry or be anxious at all, as we will get you to the airport in good time." It took me 20 minutes to pack my camera gear, and by then the plane was due to take off. I still had at least a 30-minute car drive to the airport and all my equipment to check in. On the way, worrying about my wife and the thought that the plane had left without me, I undid one of my cases, found a bottle of whisky and swigged a drop from the bottle to try and ease my tension. I arrived at the airport check-in desk to see my wife waiting anxiously for me.

The plane, with its full load of passengers, had been held up by royal command for nearly two hours. The check-in was waived and we proceeded to board the flight. When we both stepped onto the aircraft, the passengers on the flight stared at us, wondering who on earth we were. Embarrassed, we took our seats. We then took off immediately.

The following was one of the most exciting assignments of my life. I was in London when I received a telephone call. "The Shah of Iran and his family would like you to make yourself available in Teheran to photograph the family. Please let us know a date that is suitable to you." I had no idea when I caught the plane for Iran that this would turn out to be the most memorable assignment of all, for although photographers, like journalists, are used to roughing it a little when they are working abroad, I found myself plunged into the exotic and glamorous world of a powerful Imperial family.

I first met the Shah and the Empress in the candlelit drawing room in Golestan Palace. At once, I was struck by the glittering trappings of money-is-no-object opulence. From the Shah to the Empress to the courtiers who bowed in and out of the room in discreet waves, it was all like a scene from a film. It was a lovely surprise when, as they shook hands with me, they gave me a gold coin – apparently, it's a custom on New Year's Day. Salem, I believe they call it. Later I attended a formal cocktail party, followed by a magnificent dinner hosted by the Shah and his wife – this was an exhilarating and totally unexpected experience for me. The next stop was Kish, a sun-drenched island that the Shah is developing into a millionaire's playground, a sort of Monte Carlo of the Persian Gulf.

The Shah had flown in with his children the day before, piloting his own Mystère. I arrived on the Empress's flight, a Boeing 737 that was luxuriously fitted out. It belonged to the Government. At Kish airport the Empress ordered special quarters to be arranged for me.

From the moment I arrived in Kish, it was sheer luxury. My suite of rooms was in a luxurious villa. It had everything – a bulging cocktail cabinet, mounds of fruit spilling out of the most beautiful bowls, cashew nuts galore, instant service at the press of a button and, in the evenings, I had a meal cooked by a chef from the top French restaurant Maxims. What made it all particularly delightful was that my visit coincided with the Iranian New Year celebrations, and I, of course, was expected to join in.

Kish Island is off the Iranian coastline, along the eastern shores of the Persian Gulf. It is a rugged island (eight by five kilometres) being developed as a major resort with international hotels, casinos and a free-port status. Everything had to be brought from the mainland, even the drinking water. Trees had to be watered and grass was coaxed to the surface, but it had an unspoilt natural beauty and gorgeous beaches. The clear azure waters were ideal for swimming and scuba diving – if you were prepared to share it with sharks, which infest the Gulf waters. That, however, did not deter the Imperial family from visiting the island once or twice a year to stay at their beachside villa and let their hair down. At New Year two weeks were spent down at Kish, a one-and-a-half-hour jet ride from the seasonal cool of Tehran.

Kish had no mountains, not even hills. Looking out over the Persian Gulf, the imposing heights of the Iranian coastline reminded the royal holidaymakers of their tough heritage. A dhow came over the horizon and on-board the Crown Prince put on his scuba-diving gear, preparing to spear fish near the coast. On another corner of the beach the Empress came to the surface holding a shell she had found on the sea bed as she blinked excitedly in the sunlight showing off her find.

Apart from taking photographs of the Empress skiing, I took all the sporting shots on Kish including Crown Prince Reza riding his three-wheel Honda motorbike – I christened it a sand-scooter. It is not often I am able to capture pictures of a royal family at play. This family left me in no doubt that they are at their happiest when time allowed them all to be together. The overwhelming impression was of a shared love and fun; they certainly made me feel at home. The photographs that I was so excited about, and that surprised me, were of the Empress arriving in a small boat in the shark-infested waters. Dressed in scuba clothing, she dived into the blue sea. She was absolutely thrilled and enjoyed every moment as she jumped into the waters. – I said to her you wouldn't get me within a million miles of shark infested waters. Scuba diving is the sort of thing the energetic Empress does regularly. She said to me, "I find it so relaxing."

Crown Prince Reza was speeding along in his sleek Riva 2000 speed boat. I was obliged to board a flat-bottomed boat and try to keep steady as we surged across the water at speeds of up to 24 knots. This was made even more unnerving by the fact that my driver could not speak a word of

English. When I asked him to go forward he would go backwards, and vice versa, and he didn't allow for the change in the current.

When photographing Prince Reza, the Crown Prince in the Persian Gulf, it was quite harrowing. He was in a power boat, and I was at the bow as I wanted to show him at the helm with the wake behind him. To have some movement in the wake I needed to photograph the boat on the turn and going fast. I held on to the rail with one hand whilst I took photographs with the other; I was holding on for dear life, as I can't swim and the water was infested with sharks. Afterwards, when we arrived back on the beach, we sat down together, had a drink and laughed about it. It was one of the most exciting assignments I'd ever done.

However, one day it nearly ended in tragedy. The Prince was flying an F-5 fighter across the Persian Gulf. I was in the co-pilot's seat of another aircraft close by and we were speaking to each other on the radio. I would ask him to bank to the left or right or go forward or drop back – we were travelling at about 350mph and the Prince kept dipping and banking. I started taking pictures as he came nearer when suddenly I realised our wings were almost touching. I dropped my camera down at the same time as the Prince must have realised what was happening, because his jet swerved away to the right. When we landed safely a few minutes later he said to me, "You know, we nearly had it."

A burly, sports-shirted secret-service-man's walkie-talkie crackled – "Eagle to hawk. Eagle to hawk. Number three coming down the road. Number three coming to your position. Over."

"I hear you. Have spotted number three. Over."

The loud roar of three-wheeled Honda beach bikes broke the warm afternoon's silence on Kish Island. The Crown Prince and three of his friends roared at dangerous speeds down past the royal residence towards the golden sands of the Persian Gulf island's shores. An exhausted bodyguard followed the future heir, as central control helplessly tried to keep track of the Shah's eldest son. Bent over his machine in a T-shirt and jeans, the Crown Prince didn't seem to care in the least.

In the evening I was only too relieved to be able to relax in the beach restaurant, an exclusive type of club not far from the villa where the Shah's special guests gathered for dinner. It is quite near the royal villa, a tremendous place set in the most breath-taking spot. The double-glazed windows looked out over the whole area, down to the beach and the coral, where thoroughbred Arabian horses were brought for the Shah to ride in the cool evenings.

The Shah enjoyed his wife's company when they relaxed on motorbikes in the cool evenings, but he knew her real passion was skiing. When he saw my stunning skiing pictures of the Empress he said, "Her Majesty looks just like a champion."

It had been expected that His Majesty would go riding, and it was quite a sight to see the guards jumping off horses and onto any bikes they could lay their hands on. A few of the entourage even forgot to take off their riding hats. In the late afternoon the Shah mounted his grey stallion for his afternoon ride. Ten other horsemen, officers, the head of the Imperial stables and several members of his entourage rode behind him. At sunset the island and the sea in the background made a beautiful scenic view. The following afternoon the royal couple mounted their motorbikes for a spin around the island, the Shah on his 800cc Honda and the Empress on a less powerful bike. The Shah returned to the villa after a short ride, but the Empress continued with her friends. "Hit the dirt," somebody shouted as the excited group veered off the main road into the rock-strewn island terrain. A few of the party decided to get on the bus that was following. Passing the local village, the Empress stopped, turned her bike round and shouted to Princess Fatimeh that she was going to see how the villagers were. Women and children gathered around her as she listened to their requests and complaints, asking her aide to note several points. She would have the local authorities that were responsible look into those matters. She insists on prompt action and accepts no excuses.

The Shah and Empress Farah riding their motorbikes

The royal family are extremely relaxed on this holiday. The evening's programme consisted of dinner at Mohanna's, a splendid French restaurant specialising in seafood. After dinner there was a show by a popular national singer. Iranians are very sentimental people, their songs poetically emotional. Then, on to the casino that was to be visited that evening by the Their Majesties, who spent only a few minutes there. The Shah was already thinking about the dispatches and numerous reports brought in that afternoon by the daily courier. He was also receiving the American chairman of the Joint Chiefs of Staff the next morning. Affairs of state ride supreme at all times in the Shah's mind.

Meanwhile, back at the villa, the Shah was walking along in the dusk with his dog, Beno, at his side. What was going through the mind of the King of Kings at that twilight hour? "Cyrus, Great King, King of Kings, noblest of the noble, hero of the history of Iran and the world. Rest in peace, for we are awake and we will always stay awake." The Shah's voice quivered at that solemn ceremony in October 1971, the occasion on which he invoked the spirit of Cyrus the Great, the founder of the Persian monarchy and empire, 2,530 years ago, at his simple tomb at Pasargadae. "Rest in peace, for we are awake and we will always stay awake." The spirit of grandeur pervaded the millennia of a proud and rich heritage paraded in front of more than 60 heads of state: emperors, kings and queens, presidents, prime ministers, international celebrities from east and west, communists and capitalists.' They had gathered to pay homage and tribute to the Shahanshah on the occasion of the anniversary celebrations of 2,500 years of dynasty.

The Shah had shown the world that he intended to reawaken that proud heritage and create a society equal to those ruled over by Persia's legendary kings. Once he said that it was no joy to rule over a poor and backward nation. He had set about arduously rebuilding his nation. Now he could reflect and feel justly proud. Yet he is his own severest critic, as the Empress has often said, "We face numerous problems and have many shortcomings." He is a realist and a pragmatist, a diplomat in the mould of Metternich and Bismarck. He admires the strong men of history. Amongst his contemporaries, his relationship and mutual admiration for General de Gaulle was well known. "I admired Lyndon Johnson because he had the courage of his convictions and stood by them," he told me in 1969. The Shah was a man who stuck to his guns. With his growing international prestige and power, he had been forcing the world to listen to him and the world was impressed, even sometimes alarmed.

Several weeks before, in Tehran, the Empress had ordered a special helicopter to take us to Dizin to accompany her on a day of skiing in the Elburz Mountains.

Dizin is one of the more popular ski resorts, situated 60 kilometres north-east of Tehran. By car it took two hours over mountain roads. Our chopper took 15 minutes to put us down near the very small chalet that the Shah and Empress, both avid ski enthusiasts, use once or twice a week in the winter months. St. Moritz and the Villa Suvretta had not been used for over two years for security reasons. International terrorism had frightened the Swiss authorities.

The Empress waited in line at the queue for the chairlift, standing for pictures amongst skiing families who had asked her to be photographed at the top of the slope. The brilliant sunlight made the 18,000-foot peak of Mount Damavand stand out even more.

One of my favourite photos of the Empress was in a typically Iranian dress, the design of which included crystal criss-crosses on a red background. The tiara was of yellow diamonds, with a necklace and earrings to match. I must say, it was quite an anti-climax returning to England after living like a king.

Empress Farah of Iran

My next visit to Iran was my second meeting with the Shah and my fifth with the Empress. This took place in Niavaran Palace in Tehran. My pose was a formal one of the beautiful Empress Farah, when she wore a white evening gown with a neckline hem and cuffs encrusted with turquoise, as well as an eye-catching diamond and turquoise tiara with drop earrings to match. Her beautiful deep-brown eyes were her main feature and they were so expressive. The Shah was resplendent in a full white military uniform. As I began to take the photographs the Empress said, "The last time you formally photographed me it took me two hours to dress and fix my hair."

Since the temperature was now in the nineties I was, to say the least, appreciative of the time and effort Their Majesties were putting into the audience. The Shah, leaving to change out of his uniform, said "I have a lot of work in hand, I'll see you later on." And the Empress continued with the audience alone. "Turquoise and white are the national colours of Iran," she told me. "This dress material was made in Iran, although these days we do not make dress fabrics in this country."

"May I suggest you pose by the pool where the colour of the water will set off your dress" I ventured. Together we walked through the marble pillars flanking the palace entrance and down the high steps into the flower-covered grounds. We reached the pool through massive clusters of begonias and waited in the shade of a blossoming tree while an aide fetched a chair for the Empress.

From the palace to the pool was some 300 yards, and the midday temperature was now 98 degrees fahrenheit. The Empress's tiara and gown were not made for a garden stroll –. Nonetheless, she posed by the pool coolly, talking and smiling amiably. "I like the simple life. It balances the pomp and ceremony of the court. It's particularly important for me when the children are home from school because I hardly ever see them during the school term."

The children were on holiday from school, as I was to find out later that afternoon. A small golf-caddying Fiat electric car, driven by eldest son Prince Reza brought them across the grounds to the pool side. When their brother had brought the car to a halt, out jumped Princess Farahnaz, Ali Reza and baby Princess Leila. The Empress told me, "Prince Reza is an active and sometimes naughty boy. I call him 'Tootom', which in Persian means 'tobacco'."

Photographing the Shah and Empress in their private dining room at the Niavaran Palace in Tehran, I set up my equipment, then they came in and sat down. I told them what I wanted and suggested I take some pictures of them very close together as husband and wife. The Shah said, "Oh no, no, no."

I replied, "Well, look, can I show you what I would like you to do?" The Empress sat in the corner of the sofa and the Shah sat beside her and I said, "Now I want you to lean in and take his arm." But the Shah kept leaning back and pulling away from the Empress. I said, "Forget I'm here. Just be yourselves." Eventually I got the picture I wanted.

The Shah and Empress have often complained about the constraints of their positions on their family lives, that they never seemed to get enough time to spend with their children. They were both doting parents and very free in their approach to parenthood. As the Empress said, "We want them to develop their own personalities."

Persia celebrated the twenty-fifth century of its nationhood. The festivities and arrangements had been placed by the Shah into the hands of his charming wife, who told me, "It was a major event, not only for Iran but for the world. It would depict the continuity and unity of this nation over two-and-a-half thousand years – its tradition, its values and its qualities. Of course, it was a busy time for me preparing all this on top of my charitable and patronage work and my duties of state. Although it is sometimes hard, one never gives up and I always seem to find new inspiration to carry on."

The Shah and Empress are called Baba and Maman by their children – Farsi for daddy and mummy. The children do much as they please, but never beyond the patterns set by their parents. They are all very active, with the elder boy and girl looking after their younger brother and sister. The Crown Prince is a drummer and a photographer and, like his father, he loves speed and is excited by danger. He is an avid hunter and a pilot with more than 200 hours of solo flying behind him. He enjoys scuba-diving, plays tennis and skis on both snow and water. At the same time he keeps up with numerous studies, the burdens of state and functions as well as captaining his school football team. Even at an early age the Crown Prince had great poise and bore himself with dignity. He was polite and strong-willed and was known, like his father, to have a mind of his own.

When being asked to pose for a photograph behind the controls of a helicopter, he replied that he could not pilot it and therefore would not wish to be seen doing something that he could not do in reality. His sister, Princess Farahnaz, was very much like her mother, and the similarities in their nature and even tone of voice were remarkable.

As the Shah's spare time was very much restricted, the Empress was the main focus of family life. Being, herself, a warm and affectionate person, she created an atmosphere of warmth and tried as much as was humanly possible to shield the children from the pressures of public life. A recent television documentary about her daily life had her in tears as she watched herself on film putting little Princess Leila to bed. In fact the Empress had often remarked that her very sensitive nature caused much personal mental anguish as she was, every day, confronted by thousands of requests and petitions, ranging from pleas for money and favours to support for major social and cultural problems. She had been the driving force behind the government's plan to create a complete social welfare system. She was the active – chairwoman of more than 33 organisations, ranging from charities and children's books to cancer research and numerous art bodies, stemming from her interest in the arts. She had taken up the mantle of the preservation of Persian heritage, language and culture. Recently she brought back the art of passion plays, a popular religious tradition dating back centuries. The Shiraz Arts Festival, which was the brain-child of the Empress's, had become the major international cultural exchange between the east and west.

The Empress was tall, with striking dark brown eyes that sparkled with vitality. She had beautiful manners and an easy presence. She was much loved throughout the country and often travelled to the most unlikely places and kept in constant touch with the people she met. The Empress told me she was overwhelmed by the Shah's personality, and derived most of her strength from his steadfast and confident character. At times of personal or national crises it was to His Imperial Majesty that she turned to. Increasingly, she detested the profuse flattery that was the pervasive custom and tradition of kingship in Iran. She did not allow her warm and affectionate nature to interfere with the affairs of state. She has a very simple, approach to life, she is pure and authentic yet elegant and beautiful, the Empress constantly repeated that she was an ordinary girl from an ordinary background, who made good, and she never intends to forget it. "It helps me to keep things in their proper perspective," she remarked. "Sometimes, when I have an important function, audience, or an interview, I become anxious and worry that I may not be able to give of my best. However, I find that this anxiety helped me to try harder. I am a doer, and never find mental peace until I have accomplished something or righted a wrong. I couldn't bear the injustices that I saw or heard of and a mental anguish enveloped me. I was never happier than when I was amongst people – simple people – and saw their sincere and happy faces. That gave me strength and belief in God, for without it to turn to I would have been lost."

The Shah thrived on danger and loved speed. He drove at hair-raising speeds, dived out of helicopters into the sea, did 100mph on powerful motor bikes, and water-skied, drove speedboats and skied down steep slopes. He used to hunt, but for over 20 years had not done so, as he did not like the sight of blood or causing pain. In his official capacity he swore that he would never allow treason or treachery to the state to go unpunished. He pardoned those who nearly took his life, but steadfastly accepted the verdicts of executions of terrorists convicted of killing and sabotage.

In private he was a loving father, a man full of life. His hobbies, apart from sports, were a passion for bridge and a flair for backgammon. He did a great deal of reading books and periodicals of historical and contemporary interest. He loved reading history and pored over technical and specialist literature in the fields of military technology, strategy and advanced industrial technology. He read all the major international journals, magazines and newspapers early in the morning as he breakfasted on fruit-juice, coffee and toast.

His working day began at 10am on every day except Fridays, the Iranian day of rest. He received ministers and aides until 2pm and then he broke for a simple lunch, usually just with the Empress. It was here that most pertinent problems faced by them were shared. The Empress was the only person that the Shah allowed to influence him. A short nap or rest usually followed and the

Shah went to the palace gym at four in the afternoon for a daily workout. Often there were audiences in the afternoon, but the evenings were a time for rest.

The evenings were mostly for family affairs, with Saturdays and Tuesdays at the Queen Mother's house, where the whole family and friends gathered for dinner. Sundays and Wednesdays were spent at his twin sister's, Princess Ashraf, house and some Mondays at the Shah's stepsister's, Princess Fatimeh. The Shah and the Empress both loved the cinema, the Shah having a preference for light entertainment. Both liked music, though the Empress has more time for the classics. The children were television addicts and all led their own independent lives in the palace compounds. The Crown Prince lived totally separately.

That was the last time I visited Iran. From all the splendour and glitter I am now home and down to earth once again. I last met the Shah when I flew to Marrakesh in Morocco and it was there that he was granted asylum by King Hassan II. He was a dejected man, wearing a lounge-suit and reclining in a chair, reading a newspaper in the orange grove garden of his new home.

The Shah died in Panama and the Empress made her home in Connecticut, in the United States of America. This was where I last met her.

In the lounge of her new home was a coffee table, which had china bowls filled with cashew nuts and fruits. On the mantelpiece were framed photographs of her husband and children. "I don't want to live in the past," the Empress told me. "Life is about the present and the future. I will never lose my feelings for Iran, it's important I keep those feelings alive. In the earlier years of my exile I thought about my homeland and my country."

I received an invitation from Prime Minister Indira Gandhi, which I was delighted to accept, and flew to Delhi to photograph her. It was in her beautiful home in the countryside just outside of Delhi where I was welcomed as her guest for five days. Her son, Rajiv, and daughter-in-law, Sonia, and two of her grandchildren were with her. She also had, by her side, her beautiful Afghan hound, Pippa. Indira changed her sari so many times, just like a model. I even went to her office and photographed her there. She told me she usually worked a 12-hour day and sometimes all through the night. "I love working with children. I was Vice-President of the International Council for Child Welfare and when I was young I played the violin and also played chess with my husband. I am a gypsy at heart, and I have lived in England but I have never thought of London as being a beautiful city." When she was killed the whole world wanted my photographs and the German magazine *Bunte Illustrierte* flew their private jet to London to obtain them.

Indira Ghandi

Another important news story was in Venice in 1961, where my wife and I were on holiday. We went down to the beach on the lido and I could not believe that there before me sat The Duke of Windsor and his wife, Wallis Simpson. I jumped up from my deckchair, passing them en–route, went back to my hotel room and brought my cameras down to the beach. I photographed them like a paparazzi as they reclined in their chairs and went down to the sea to snorkel. I got the most unbelievable results, which paid for our holiday. A few years later I photographed them officially in their home in the Bois de Bolougne in Paris, where they relaxed and reclined on their terrace.

Duke and Duchess of Windsor

I was invited to photograph the wife of the President of France, Madame Valéry Giscard d'Estaing in the Élysée Palace in Paris. The grandeur of the palace rooms, in pale blue and gold, and heavily mirrored doors was extremely ornate. She posed for me in a brilliant red dress, very formally as she sat on a settee. She then changed into a paisley style dress and leaned against the Victorian marble fireplace, where on the mantelpiece stood a huge ormolu clock and twin candelabras. We then went out into the grounds of the palace where she walked her black labrador dog. All the photographs appeared on the cover and inside the French magazine *Paris Match*.

Anne-Aymone Giscard d'Estaing

Cascais in Portugal is a beautiful coastal resort where I travelled to photograph former King Umberto of Italy. This was where he made his home after being exiled. He welcomed me to his beautiful villa that overlooked the sea. He was an extremely tall and slender man, very immaculate in dress and dignified in appearance. I was amazed at the size of his library and his wonderful collection of books. "My main hobby is reading. I have been exiled a very long time and I doubt whether Italy will ever again become a monarchy. I live here by the sea, which I thoroughly enjoy," he told me. We drank a glass of white wine before I left for the one-hour journey back to the airport at Lisbon.

It was Princess Ira von Fürstenberg who I photographed in Venice in her aunt's home in a village called Mestre. We took lunch at the famous Cipriano's, on the waterway, the day before shooting. I was with her for some five hours, taking photographs inside the villa and in an archway of flowers in the garden. She is the only person I have ever photographed in a bath. Mind you, she was covered in foam, which I had purchased from a local chemist the day before, but it was certainly an unusual setting. At the end of the session I was truly worn out and we had a spaghetti meal at the Bauer Hotel on the lake. The following day I photographed the Princess on a gondola. She held a parasol and the gondolier serenaded her as he wove his way through the Venetian waterways. She flew to London to see the results and was delighted with what she saw. We had lunch once again in an Italian restaurant in the city.

Princess Ira Fürstenberg

I flew to New York for a photo session with Ingrid Bergman's daughter, Isabella Rossellini. She was the Lancôme girl who took over from Princess Ira Fürstenberg. Isabella was wonderful to photograph and I could see her resemblance to her mother. She posed for me in a grey/blue satin gown and used the same material for a turban which made her look like Joan of Arc, the magazine editors said.

Isabella Rossellini

Another famous person I photographed was Ratna Seri Dewi Sukarno, the wife of the President of Indonesia. She was originally a geisha girl, a very beautiful raven-haired petite woman. That was in Paris and I was with her for 11 hours. We even went to a Japanese restaurant where she posed in a kimono. My wife, who accompanied me to Paris, was extremely worried about me as she waited alone in the hotel as I had been absent from her for so long.

As the private audiences were exclusive, there was no need to rush distribution and I could take my time. However, on an important news event such as the death of the Shah of Iran, magazines worldwide were immediately demanding my photographs. On that particular occasion my wife flew to Paris to see editors and I flew to Hamburg to do the same.

In the early years before digital photography came into existence, all the photographs taken overseas on state visits had to be handled at speed. The photographs were forwarded to the nearest airport by courier and the package of films was put on an aircraft and freighted to London. There it was collected and taken to my wife who dealt with the processing. She would then select the pictures and distribute them to magazines all over the world. My wife, Audrey, has been a great help in my career. She acted as my secretary, my adviser, and my severest critic. Without her I would have been lost; we were a great team. I would arrive home from an overseas trip and there would be no pictures for me to see. They had already been syndicated. Speed was of the most importance. It must have been very hard for her working at home whilst I jetted from country to country. However, she distributed to the magazines from whom I had been commissioned, and I would not see any results of my work for several months until publication. Once the photographs had been returned to us after publication, they would then be catalogued and put into the library.

I checked into the Beverly Wilshire Hotel when I first arrived in Los Angeles. It was there that I set up my base to meet some of the actresses of Hollywood. The meeting point to see anybody was either at hotel bar or the coffee shop. I had been talking to someone who introduced me to the publicist of the Ford motor company. For the three-week period that I was in Los Angeles they gave me the use of a brand new blue convertible Ford Galaxy car. After making many telephone calls I was invited to the Warner Bros.' studios and there was introduced to Carroll Baker who was making the film Harlow about the famous actress Jean Harlow.

I photographed her on-set, laying on a chaise longue, and I was given the facility of using the studio lighting at will. The pictures were marvellous. I was then invited to her home and took a series of shots of her with her family – her husband, Jack, and two children. She was so professional to work with. I then had a phone call from Natalie Wood's agent who invited me to take pictures of her. I declined because she wanted the films processed in Los Angeles; I insisted that I had to have my films processed at my own laboratory in London. Next I met the dancer Dorothy Provine and later, Joan Collins.

Dame Joan Collins

I took photographs of Joan in her home in Los Angeles, but prior to doing so she made me sign a contract that none of my pictures could be published in the American magazine National Enquirer. Why, I had no idea. Nonetheless, the magazine supplied the gowns for me in which to photograph her and she accepted to be photographed in them, knowing who had supplied them. Before any of those pictures were released I went to her home in Maida Vale for her viewing. I must say, she makes herself up beautifully, but when I saw her at the time of the viewing, it was a completely different woman that I saw in front of me. It was her natural self. I was rather surprised seeing her without make-up, but she still had that glamorous and vivacious glow about her.

Well, today was the day – my big day – and I had been nervously waiting for the hours to pass. My beautiful daughter, Marilyn, and my son-in-law, Jonathan, called for my wife, Audrey, and me at 8.30am – and we were both ready to leave. The traffic was moving at a snail's pace and was very heavy-going towards town. I was anxiously looking at my watch, hoping we would arrive at the palace in plenty of time. Arriving at the palace gates, the heavy police security inspected our car. The bonnet and boot were searched and we then proceeded to the gate, where we had to produce our passports and our entry card for identification. We drove through the southern gate into the forecourt, through the arch and into the quadrangle. We had arrived.

We alighted from the car and proceeded into the palace and up the grand staircase. As the recipient of the award, I had to go in one direction and my three guests went in another. I proceeded into an enormous portrait gallery and was then directed into a further room to join all the other recipients.

We were informed by a senior military officer, in a very formal manner, what the procedure was. The men would have to bow their heads while the ladies would have to curtsy. He demonstrated the actions as he informed us, and it was quite amusing.

During this time, my guests were ushered by a military officer to their seats in the ballroom where the investiture would take place. On the balcony was the orchestra, the Band of the Blues and Royals. The first piece of music they played was a suite by Bach. During this period I chatted with another recipient who was also receiving an MBE and we both tried to calm each other's nerves. It was now 10.40am and the Queen was not due to arrive on the dais until precisely 11.00am.

The format was that, when his or her name was called, each recipient joined the line that would start the walk to the large gilded open doors, eventually leading into the ballroom. As one moved closer to the doors, I had the first glimpse of the Queen and the adrenalin started to flow. I could hear the music being played, changing from *Ave Maria* to *My Fair Lady,* as I moved up to the Admiral, who was in position at my last stop to usher me to Her Majesty. My name was announced, "Reginald Davis, for services to photography and charity." I took three paces and turned and walked to the dais where in front of me was Her Majesty. I bowed, looked at her from some 18 inches away and said, "Your Majesty."

She replied, "How are you and how is your charity doing?"

I said, "I am showing all the photographs of your family over the years, Ma'am, and it is going very well." I told her she looked very good and she extended her hand to shake hands, saying, "Congratulations, take care." With that, I backed away, bowed again and left the room to the music of *My Fair Lady.*

At the end of the ceremony, at exactly 12 noon, the Queen, who had been standing for all that time, proceeded out of the ballroom followed by two Gurkha Orderly Officers and five Yeomen of the Guard. I then rejoined my family and we proceeded to the quadrangle for photographs. What a wonderful, exciting, exhilarating and historic day.

I eventually gave up the hustle and bustle of the royal tours and state visits that had spanned over 35 years. For the younger man it was very interesting and often exciting seeing many parts of the world and attending banquets, balls, openings of parliaments and press receptions to meet and talk with the royals during off-duty periods. The carrying of the heavy camera equipment, and the jostling with the police, the public and the sometimes strong arms of security were not so great – thank goodness those days are over. Once you had covered one royal tour, all were alike. It was true, the places were different, but the routine was virtually the same – the arrivals, the meetings, the walkabouts, the banquets and the farewells.

On state visits I had to change clothing several times, from lounge suit during the day to dinner jacket and even white tie and tails in the evening. I remember, in Washington, I ordered a sandwich and a beer to be sent to my room as I changed. I had to try and eat and drink whilst dressing and even then I couldn't finish my 'gourmet meal' but had to dash to catch the transport to the next venue. The rush in having to send films back to base and the quick re-loading of my equipment was no joke either. The enjoyment of a tour was the company of colleagues and the wisecracking and fun we made ourselves. When I was with a colleague in Hamilton near Niagara, photographing Princess Anne who was giving a speech in the open air, it began to rain. To make matters worse, a heavy mist came down that obscured everything. "I can't see a thing!" my colleague next to me shouted, peering hopelessly into his camera.

I shouted back, "Nor can I."

The Princess in front of us could hear our chat and shouted back, "Shut up, I can hear you!" We laughed.

I found a lot of excitement in my work, which I wouldn't have missed for anything. I have flown in a helicopter, photographing Churchill's funeral. I've flown in Air Force One, been driven in a power-boat with the Crown Prince of Iran and privately dined with royalty. I have also received many gifts, including being decorated, all because I was a photographer. I can now look back over those years and realise how lucky I was to have had a profession that gave me and many others great pleasure.

Over the many years my work has appeared in *The Daily Mail, The Daily Express, The Daily Mirror, The Daily Telegraph, The Observer, The Sunday Times, The Sunday Mirror, The Mail on Sunday, Hello, OK, Queen Magazine, Woman's Own, Woman, Woman's Journal, Woman's Mirror, Country Life, Look, People, Newsweek, National Enquirer, Toronto Star* (Canada), *Paris Match* (France), *Jours de France* (France), *Point de Vue* (France), *Le Figaro* (France), *Madame Figaro* (France), *Oggi* (Italy), *Libelle* (Holland), *Margriet* (Holland), *Svensk Damtidning* (Sweden) *Bunte Illustrierte* (Germany), *Freizeit Revue* (Germany), *Quick,* (Germany) *Neue Post, Germany Neue Welt Germany, Das Neue Blatt* (Germany), *Anna* (Finland), *Bild* (Denmark), *Norsk Ukeblad, Australian Women's Weekly, Australian Woman's Day, Women's Weekly* (New Zealand), *Schwiezer Illustrierte (Switzerland), Fair Lady* (South Africa), and *Holla* (Spain).

Today I am retired at the young age of 92. Why not? But I still carry on releasing my pictures for publication worldwide from the library which I started in the 1950s. The excitement is still there when I see a publication in a newspaper or magazine with my name beneath it. I have many cuttings of past publications that fill several cupboards. I can now sit back and remember all the hard and exhausting work over so many years, and those wonderful, exciting times I had the good fortune to have had.